Beyond the Pale

★

THIS BOOK is a Who's Brew of the beer world. Every British light ale, best bitter, and sweet stout can be found within these pages, together with a generous selection of brews from elsewhere in the world. If you want to know who brews Draught Excluder, tap this Dictionary for the answer.

Of course, time and fermentation wait for no writer. Between the final draft being spilt over the bar, and publication, not only will new brews have been born and old ales passed away, but also whole breweries boarded up and closed down.

After a few years' phoney peace, a strong takeover tide is ripping again through the British brewing industry. As I write, a bitter battle is raging to save Matthew Brown's Lion Ales of Blackburn from the clutches of Scottish & Newcastle Breweries. Meanwhile, within the national combines, rationalisation is the order of the dray. One moment in 1985 Watney's Norwich Brewery was in production; the next its insides are gutted. All these developments mean less choice for the drinker.

At the opposite end of the brewhouse ladder, a fresh feast of local ales has frothed up in the past decade. But brewing has proved a hard business to enter; most pubs are tied to the national concerns, with the result that many of the pioneers of this brave new world have, sadly, gone to the brewhouse wall. On the brighter side of the glass, there are still bold ventures rolling out their first barrel every month. But how long will this continue when the trade is closed in their face?

Thus beer is in every sense liquid. You can't pin it down. Change is on the boil all the time. But this Dictionary will give you the chance to taste the wide variety of British beer still surviving, from milds to barley wines. Every brand is included here.

Even that drink in which we are all in danger of drowning – lager – the golden dream of the marketing men and brewery accountants, is covered. And we have not stopped at the White Cliffs of Dover. You can discover true Continental lagers and other more distinctive beer styles from around the world inside these pages.

The Dictionary also attempts to explain the many technical terms used in the brewing industry, from alpha acid to zymurgy, without requiring a master's degree in chemistry. A few slang words slipped through as well to add a little spice. We hope you like the recipe.

But, above all, don't delay your sampling in and out of this book – or you could miss some fine brews. Not only are many breweries in danger of disappearing, and cask milds in general under threat, but also a number of companies have recently stopped bottling – like Brakspears, Hydes, and Jennings – while others have cut back their range of special beers.

Stouts in particular are looking thin. Marston's Mello and Robinson's Unicorn are just two that have vanished. At the same time, Whitbread's Gold Label has been busy elbowing rival barley wines off the shelf, like Greene King's Audit and Morland's Monarch.

So dip into these pages and try something different – you might just be in time to save an endangered species.

Brian Glover
May 1985

CAMRA

DICTIONARY OF

BEER

Brian Glover

Longman

Longman Group Limited,
Longman House, Burnt Mill, Harlow,
Essex CM20 2JE, England
and Associated Companies throughout the world.

© Longman Group Limited 1985
First published 1985

British Library Cataloguing in Publication Data

Glover, Brian
  CAMRA dictionary of beer.
  1. Beer
  I. Title II. Campaign for Real Ale
  641.2'3 TP577

  ISBN 0-582-89261-9

Set in 9/11 Quadritek Garamond with Univers
Extra Bold by John Hills Typesetting Limited,
Sawbridgeworth, Herts.
Printed in Great Britain
by Spottiswoode Ballantyne Ltd.,
Colchester and London

★ *How to use this book* ★

The Dictionary lists every British brewery and all the beers they currently produce. Beers with the same name as the brewery, e.g. Boddingtons Bitter, are mentioned only under the brewery entry. Beers with a distinctive name, e.g. Ruddles County, are mentioned both under the beer's own title (County) and the brewery (Ruddles). Thus, if you want to know who brews a beer, look under the beer's name – and then cross-check for more information under the brewery.

After each British beer an Original Gravity figure (e.g. 1037) is given, indicating its strength. Original Gravity is the measure of the amount of fermentable material added to water (rated at 1000 degrees) to make beer. A 1037 beer thus has 37 parts of fermentable material to every 1000 parts of water. How far this 'body' turns to alcohol depends on how far the beer is fermented out. A very rough rule of thumb says that every ten degrees equals one per cent alcohol. The average British bitter has an OG of 1035-40, about 3.5-4 per cent alcohol.

Cask beers are listed first under each brewery, in ascending order of strength, followed by keg (including lager), and then bottled. Canned beers are included only where they are distinct brews from keg or bottled. Again, cross-refer from a brewery to a beer listing for further information.

The only beers with distinctive names not listed separately are those unique brews belonging to home-brew pubs. These are just mentioned under the home-brew pub entry, since they are sold only on the premises.

A sample of well-known or distinctive foreign beers and breweries is also included. The alcohol percentage figures given after such beers are alcohol by volume.

Many brewing and bar terms are also listed, while avoiding the wide range of archaic names which are no longer used. The aim is to provide an up-to-date dictionary. Pub games and cider have not been mixed in, since each could make a dictionary on their own.

Acknowledgements

This book is not the work of one tired brain, but the result of the efforts of many sharper ones. Above all, I must thank Pat O'Neill and Tony Millns of CAMRA's Technical Committee for supplying the bulk of the brewing terms. If the deadline had been any longer, Pat would have filled another 30 pages. Peter Lerner of the Pub Preservation Group pitched in with pub items; Tim Webb and Danny Blyth amazed me and shocked many more with their knowledge of basic bar slang, only a small part of which can, fortunately, be included here; while Jo Bates provided a skilled accompaniment on keyboard. And I would have been lost outside these shores without the guidance of Michael Jackson's excellent books, notably his *World Guide to Beer*. Last but not least, I must thank the many CAMRA members and brewery staff who helped, directly or indirectly, in supplying information on British breweries and beers.

[A]

Abbaye Strictly speaking, this powerful Continental style should apply only to the very strong, top-fermenting beers, naturally-conditioned in the bottle, produced by five Trappist abbeys in Belgium and another across the Dutch border (see *Trappist*). But many similar 'abbaye' brews are made by conventional Belgian breweries. A dozen German abbeys also brew their own beer, but without a distinctive style.

Abbey Small brewery near Retford, Notts, set up in 1981. May move to Herefordshire. *Cask beers*: Bitter (1036), Supreme (1043). Abbey Brewery is also the name of Scottish & Newcastle's head offices in Edinburgh.

Abbey Ale Strong cask beer (1047) from Cirencester Brewery, Glos. Also Shepherd Neame keg (1039) and bottled beer (1045) from Kent.

Abbot Greene King's famous full-bodied ale (1048) from East Anglia, available in cask, keg, and bottle. Originally introduced in 1951 to relieve pressure on the bottling hall by encouraging sales of draught beer through a quality product!

ABC Aylesbury Brewery Company, or ABC as it is popularly known, ceased brewing in 1935, but still runs 200 pubs around Buckinghamshire. Merged with Allied in 1972. Cask ABC Bitter (1037) is brewed by Ind Coope in Burton.

Abington Clifton Inns home-brew pub in Northampton. *Cask beers*: Cobblers (1037), Extra (1047).

Abt The strongest Belgian ale (12 per cent alcohol), produced in the Trappist style by the abbey of St Sixtus at Westvleteren. Besides Abt (abbot) there are also, in descending order of holiness and strength, Prior and Pater.

Ace Keg lager (1032) from Federation of Newcastle. Ace of Clubs is also the sign of this northeast clubs brewery.

Acetic Acid The acid giving the sourness to vinegar. Acetic acid is the breakdown product of the oxidation of alcohol, most easily brought about by the action of the bacterium Acetobacter, which is ever-present in the air. Any beer left exposed to air will eventually turn into a malt vinegar.

Adelscott A novelty beer from the French Adelshoffen brewery (part of the Pêcheur group), which claims to be 'Bière au Malt à Whisky' since it is brewed from malt kilned with peat.

Adjunct Material added to malted barley to make up a cheaper grist, notably flaked maize, rice, or wheat, or various sugars.

Admiral's Ale Cask premium bitter (1048) from Southsea Brewery, Portsmouth.

Adnams Independent Suffolk company serving real ale in all 68 tied houses. Famous for its bitter, which has proved so popular in the free trade that the seaside brewery has been expanded, though horse-drawn drays still deliver around Southwold. *Cask beers*: Mild (1034), Bitter (1036), Old (1042). *Bottled*: Champion (1032), Nut Brown (1034), Fisherman (1042), Broadside (1068), Tally Ho (1075).

Ailric's Cask old ale (1045) from Phillips, Bucks.

Air Pressure Beer dispense system which involves the application of compressed air onto the surface of the beer in the cask, forcing the beer up to the counter through an extractor syphon. The system is little-used in England but still common in Scotland, where it operates in conjunction with *Tall Founts*. Air pressure helps to maintain good condition in the beer.

AK Popular cask mild (1033) from McMullen of Hertford and light bitter (1036) from Simpkiss of the Black Country. And still no one's sure what the initials mean.

Albion Marston's keg mild (1030) and bitter (1037) from Burton-upon-Trent.

Alcohol Common or ethyl alcohol is the main intoxicating component in fermented drinks; it is a waste product of the digestion of sugar by yeast. Other varieties of alcohol can also be produced in small quantities, and the concentrations of these can markedly increase the after-effects of over-indulgence.

Alcohol Content The amount of alcohol contained in a drink. This can be specified in a variety of ways: directly in percentage by weight or volume (not the same, since alcohol is lighter than water), in several systems of 'degrees' – degrees proof, degrees Plato, degrees Balling – or indirectly by quoting the original gravity.

Alcoholic (1) Containing or relating to alcohol. **(2)** Someone suffering from alcoholism, the addiction to alcoholic drink. The medical evidence is conflicting as to whether this disorder is primarily physiological or psychological.

Alcoholics Anonymous Alcoholics Anonymous (AA) is a grouping of alcoholism sufferers who meet for self-help in counselling and group therapy. The organisation has branches in most sizeable towns.

Alderney Ale Malt extract brew (1035) from the Braye Brewery on the Channel Island of Alderney.

Ale A type of beer fermented with the top-fermentation ale yeast, *Saccharomyces cerevisiae*. In Anglo-Saxon times, the words 'beor' (beer) and 'ealu' (ale) were interchangeable. Divergence in meaning occurred in the late 16th century, when 'ale' came to imply an alcoholic drink made from malt without hops, and 'beer' implied the hopped beverage. This distinction is still implicit in current phrases such as 'mild ale' (not 'mild beer'), but 'ale' does not now imply that the drink is unhopped.

Alexandra Rapidly expanding Brighton brewery set up in 1982, which owns seven pubs with many more on the way. Trades under the name of Becket's bars and ales. *Cask beers*: Becket's Mild (1033), Bitter (1036), Best (1043), Special (1047), Old Snowy (1054). *Keg*: 1066 (1064).

Alford Arms Whitbread home-brew pub (using malt extract) at Frithsden, Herts. *Cask beers*: Cherrypicker's (1036), Strong Amber (1044), Rudolf's Revenge

(1055).

Alice Ambitious new brewery to serve the Scottish Highlands, set up in Inverness in 1983. Its cask beers are often pressurised. *Cask*: Alice Ale (1040), Sixty (1060). *Keg*: Longman Lager (1040). *Bottled*: 80/- Export (1040).

Allbright Welsh Brewers keg bitter (1033), and Mitchells & Butlers bottled beer (1040).

Allied Breweries Formed in 1961 through the merger of Ind Coope, Ansells, and Tetley Walker to create Britain's largest drinks group. In 1978 merged with food firm Joe Lyons to form Allied Lyons. Runs six main breweries in Burton, Romford, Leeds, Warrington, Alloa, and Wrexham. Control of its 7,000 pubs has been decentralised to 25 trading companies, often under old brewery names like Benskins, Friary Meux, and Taylor Walker in the southeast, Halls in the southwest, Holt, Plant & Deakin in the West Midlands and Peter Walker in the northwest. Also owns 800 Victoria Wine off-licences, Coates-Gaymer cider, Teacher's whisky, Harvey's sherry etc., plus two Dutch breweries, a third of the Guinness-controlled Irish Ale Breweries (Smithwicks etc) and 20 per cent of Castlemaine-Tooheys in Australia.

All Nations Historic home-brew house in Madeley, Shropshire. One of only four left in the country by the early 1970s. *Cask beer*: Pale Ale (1032).

Alloa Scottish arm of Allied Breweries, which in 1980 became the 'third force' in Scotland with the purchase of 220 pubs from Vaux. Once largely a lager brewery, it now brews its own real ale for 35 of its 242 houses. *Cask beer*: Arrol's 70/- (1037). *Keg*: Original Light (1032), Original Pale (1032), Diamond Heavy (1036), Export (1042), Skol (1037). *Canned*: As keg.

Allsopp One of the historic names in British brewing: founded at Burton in 1709, it merged with Ind Coope in

1934, and traded as Ind Coope Allsopp until 1959. Name revived for Allied's East Midlands and East Anglia company in 1985. Also used for keg and bottled export lager (1046).

Almond Former brewery near Wigan taken over by Burtonwood in 1968 and used as a wine and spirit company. However, in 1984 Burtonwood revived the name for a few pubs and introduced a hoppier version of their own bitter, called Almond's Best Bitter (1036.5).

Alpha Acid The main component of the bitter flavour in the hop flower, contained in the alpha resin. Hops are often ranked by their alpha acid content. Hops with a very high alpha acid content can, however, be somewhat coarse in bitterness, lacking the balance of subtle flavours from the other bittering components. See *Hop*.

Alt German beer style centred on Düsseldorf in the northwest. The word means old, since the copper-coloured beer is brewed by the ancient top-fermentation method. Alt is thus a rare German ale, not a lager. The commonest brand is Hannen. Düsseldorf boasts four home-brew houses specialising in Alt, notably Zum Uerige.

Amber Whitbread's weak keg beer (1033) for Wales and the northwest. Also Newcastle's 'other' bottled beer (1033) and one by Crown (1033).

Amber malt Specially malted barley that is added to a pre-heated kiln and slowly allowed to cool in order to attain the desired colour.

Amboss Hydes keg lager (1036) from Manchester. The name is German for 'anvil', the brewery's tradename.

Amstel Famous Dutch brewery which was taken over by its Amsterdam rival, Heineken, in 1968. Main beers are a basic Pils and premium Gold. Also brewed under licence in Greece, South Africa, and the Middle East.

Anchor Strong keg and canned export beer (1048) from North Country Breweries of Hull. More surprisingly, the name of Gibbs Mew's landlocked brewery in Salisbury, Wiltshire, and their keg bitter (1039).

Anchor Steam This small San Francisco company is the only brewery in the world producing two classics,

Anchor Steam Beer and Porter, by the unique American fermentation method of long shallow pans called clarifiers. The pressure released when the casks are tapped is said to have given the lively beer its 'steam' tag.

Ancient Druids First home-brew pub (using malt extract) set up by a regional brewery, Charles Wells of Bedford, in 1984 in Cambridge. *Cask beers*: Kite Bitter (1038), Druids Special (1045).

Andover Ale Cask beer (1040) from Bourne Valley Brewery, Hampshire.

Angler Bottled strong lager (1054) for export from Charles Wells of Bedford.

Anglian Norwich strong keg and bottled ale (1048).

Anheuser-Busch The world's largest brewing company – four times the size of Britain's biggest brewer – based in St Louis, Missouri, producing the well-known Budweiser. Altogether it has 11 plants in the United States, with the bulk of its 50 million barrels a year sold in North America. Besides 'Bud', it also produces a premium lager called Michelob.

Anker A ten-gallon cask. Very rare, although ten gallons is a common size for kegs.

Ann Street Channel Island brewery in St Helier, Jersey, producing no real ale but keg and bottled beers under the brand name Mary Ann, plus a stronger version of Skol lager under licence from Allied Breweries. The brewery owns 49 pubs in Jersey. *Keg beers*: Bitter (1034), Special (1044), Skol (1040). *Bottled*: Pale Ale (1034), Brown Ale (1036), Stout (1038), Special (1044), Skol (1044), Jubilee (1064).

Ansells Birmingham brewery which merged with Ind Coope and Tetley in 1961 to form Allied Breweries – and 20 years later lost its Aston brewery. All Ansells beers are now brewed at Burton for their 1,400 pubs, half of which are run by five subsidiary companies: Ansells Burslem (Potteries); Holt, Plant & Deakin (Black Country); Lloyd & Trouncer (North Wales); Georges (West Wales); Ansells Cambrian (South Wales). *Cask beers*: Mild (1035.5), Bitter (1037). *Keg*: As cask, plus Pale (1033).

Antler Watney's value-for-money cask and keg bitter (1035).

Anvil Beers from Hydes of Manchester, notably Anvil Strong Ale (1080), a rich winter brew.

Archer (**1**) Lees bottled stout (1042) from Manchester. (**2**) The symbol of Home Brewery of Nottingham.

Archers Successful new brewery set up in Swindon in 1979 which recently expanded production to meet free-trade demand. Owns two tied houses. *Cask beers*: Village (1035), Best Bitter (1040), Golden (1050), Headbanger (1065).

Archway Cask bitter (1042) from the Tooley Street Brewery in the railway arches next to the London Dungeon.

Arctic Lite Allied's low-carbohydrate lager (1032) from Burton.

Argyle Small Edinburgh brewery originally established in 1982 as the Leith Brewery. *Cask beer*: Argyle 80/- (1043).

Arkell Swindon family brewery since 1843, serving real ale in 53 of its 64 pubs, under the sign of the 'Ark'. *Cask beers*: John Arkell Bitter (1033), BBB (1038), Kingsdown Ale (1050). *Keg*: North Star Bitter (1036), Kellar Lager (1033), 1843 Lager (1042). *Bottled*: Light Ale (1033), BBB (1038), Kingsdown (1050). See also *Donnington*.

Arrol Archibald Arrol 70/- (1037) is the sole real ale from Allied's Alloa Brewery in Scotland. Named after the brewery's founder.

Artist (**1**) Slang term for an experienced drinker. (**2**) The symbol of Morland's Abingdon brewery and the name of their light keg beer (1032).

Artists Ale Paradise Brewery's premium cask bitter (1055) from Cornwall.

Ashford New brewery set up in Kent in 1983. *Cask beers*: Kentish Gold (1035), Challenger (1039), Old Gold (1047).

Aspirating Valve See *Cask Breather*.

Aston Manor Ambitious Birmingham brewery set up in 1983, concentrating on supplying bottled beer to wholesalers and supermarkets. Also owns two pubs and two clubs, with more on the way. *Cask beers*: Mild (1035), Bitter (1038). *Keg*: As cask. *Bottled*: Mild (1031), Bitter (1031), Lager (1031) – imported from Belgium.

Attemperation Controlling the temperature at which the fermentation of beer takes place. This temperature is very important – too low and the fermentation may stop ('stick'); too high and it may 'race', producing coarse flavours. Many fermenting vats are fitted with attemperation coils through which suitably cold or warm water can be circulated to control the temperature of the fermenting wort.

Attenuate The attenuation of a beer is the extent to which the fermentable sugars have been used up by the yeast; no beer ever has the sugars used up entirely. Highly attenuated beers have a very dry palate; less attenuation yields a sweet beer.

Augustiner The oldest brewery in Munich, noted for its adjoining beer garden. It was originally part of a monastery, and there is still a monastic brewery called Augustiner over the Austrian border in Salzburg.

Autovac See *Economiser*.

Auxiliary See *LVA*.

Axe Vale Small brewery set up in Colyton, Devon, in 1983, serving 25 outlets. *Cask beers*: Bitter (1040), Battleaxe (1053), Conqueror (1066).

Ayingerbrau Sam Smith's 'Bavarian' keg lager (1039) from Tadcaster, Yorkshire. Also stronger D Pils (1047) and, in bottle only, Ayingerbrau Special (1081).

Aylesbury Brewery See *ABC*.

[B]

Badger Beers from Hall & Woodhouse of Dorset, notably Badger Best cask bitter (1041). There's even a Brock Lager in the set.

Baileys Small brewery near Malvern in Worcestershire, set up in 1983 and serving 35 outlets. *Cask beers*: Best Bitter (1040), Super Brew (1047).

Ballantine The most notable (and obscure) of America's East Coast ales, brewed by Falstaff's Narrangansett brewery in Cranston, Rhode Island. IPA (1076) or Brewer's Gold (1070) are the beers to find, having been aged in wood for 4-5 months. The basic Ballantine's Ale is much blander.

Ballard's Small country brewery on the Sussex/ Hampshire border, set up in 1980. *Cask beers*: Best Bitter (1042), Wassail (1060).

Bamberg The Bavarian home of 'smoked' beer. See *Rauchbier.*

Banks & Taylor Small Bedfordshire brewery set up in Shefford in 1981, now with four tied houses. *Cask beers*: Shefford Bitter (1038), Eastcote Ale (1041), SOS (1050).

Banks's With Hanson's makes up the large West Midlands company of Wolverhampton and Dudley Breweries which has now expanded as far afield as Bristol, Derby, and Manchester. All 700-plus pubs serve cask beer from electric pumps under  the slogan 'Unspoilt by Progress' – with mild the best seller! *Cask beers*: Mild (1036), Bitter (1038). *Keg*: Lion Mild (1035), Bitter (1037). *Bottled*: Mild (1035), Special Bitter (1035), Pale Ale (1037), Imperial Old Ale (1096).

Bar (1) A public room within a pub, as in Public Bar. (2) Often personalised name for a hostelry, especially in Scotland and Ireland, as in Bennet's Bar. (3) A division between customers and staff, where drinks are served, more properly described as a bar counter. **(4)** Bad news – 'You're barred!'. Licensees have an absolute right to bar anyone they choose from their pub.

Barbican Bass's alcohol-free lager which is distilled to remove the alcohol.

Barley Cereal crop belonging to the Graminae family of grasses, from which malt is made for brewing.

Barleycorn Hall's keg pale ale (1033) brewed in Burton.

Barley Wine A strong, rich, and sweetish ale, usually over 1060 OG, dark in colour, with high condition and a high hop rate. Extended fermentation times render most barley wines potent in alcohol; for this reason, and because of their heavy palate, they are usually sold in 'nip' bottles containing one-third of a pint. Whitbread's Gold Label is probably the most common example.

Barm The frothy yeast head that rises to the top of a fermenting vessel. 'Barmy beer' used to be an expression for young beer, still fermenting; hence 'barmy' came to be used to describe someone lightheaded or frothy.

Barnstormer Stallion's strong ale (1048) from Cippenham, Berks.

Barrel A 36-gallon cask. Not a general name for any other size; the general term is *Cask*.

Barrelage The usual way of describing a pub's (or brewery's) business in barrels (36 gallons) per week or per year.

Barrelage Agreement A common method for a brewery to tie up a so-called 'free' outlet – in return for a 'cheap' loan, the pub or club agrees to buy a certain annual barrelage.

Barron Tenth new brewery in Devon, set up in 1984 in Silverton. *Cask beer*: Barron's Draught (1040).

Bartlett Home-brewed cask beers at the Tavern, Newnham Bridge, Worcs: Mild (1040), Bitter (1042).

Bass Britain's biggest brewers, based in Burton, now controlling 20% of the industry. Merged with Burton rivals, Worthington, in 1927; with Midland rivals Mitchells & Butlers in 1961; and with Charrington in 1967.

Run 13 breweries in Burton, Birmingham, Walsall, Wolverhampton, Runcorn, Alton, Sheffield (2), Tadcaster, Cardiff, Glasgow, Edinburgh, and Belfast, and 7,500 pubs. Also have major stakes in Higsons, Castletown, and Maclays. Other interests include Crest Hotels, Corals, Pontins, Hedges & Butler, and Canada Dry. Their famous national cask beer, Draught Bass (1044), is slowly returning to its former character after ceasing to be brewed on the Burton Union system in 1982.

Bass Ale Bass keg bitter (1036) for Ireland from its Ulster brewery.

Bass North Bass company responsible for Northern England, with five trading regions: Bass Lancashire, Northwest, Northeast, Yorkshire, and Stones and four breweries at Runcorn, Tadcaster, and Sheffield (2). All cask beer is brewed at Tadcaster apart from Stones. *Cask beers*: Best Mild (1031), Extra or Toby Light (1031), Tower or Cask Bitter (1036), Blackpool Best Mild (1036). *Keg*: Best Mild (1031), Extra or Toby Light (1031), North Eastern (1032), Brew Ten (1036). See also *Stones*.

Bass Special Tennent Caledonian's keg ale (1035) in Scotland.

Bateman Lincolnshire family brewery serving 'Good Honest Ales' to its 104 Fenland pubs from its Wainfleet brewery. Famous for its windmill landmark and powerful XXXB. *Cask beers*: Mild (1032), XB (1036), XXXB (1048). *Keg*: Mild (1033), Bitter (1037). *Bottled*: Nut Brown (1033), Double Brown (1037), IPA (1037), Ploughman's Ale (1049).

Bates Small brewery set up in Bovey Tracey, South Devon, in 1983, serving 20 outlets. *Cask beer*: Bates Bitter (1045).

Batham Small Black Country family brewery with eight pubs, which brews its distinctive beers behind one of the most remarkable brewery taps in Britain, the Vine or 'Bull and Bladder' in Brierley Hill which declares across its front 'Blessing of your heart, you brew good ale'.

Cask beers: Mild (1036), Bitter (1043), Delph Strong Ale (1054).

Battersea Watney pub brewery, Prince of Wales, Battersea. *Cask beers*: Bitter (1036), Best Bitter (1040), Power House (1050).

Battleaxe Strong cask ale (1053) from Axe Vale brewery, Devon.

BB Initials usually given to light West Country bitters from breweries like Palmers (1030.4) and St Austell (1031). Popularly known as 'Boys Bitter'. Also a weak Whitbread keg beer (1031) for the Luton area. Occasionally means 'Best Bitter', as in the BB produced by Harveys of Lewes, Sussex.

BBA Best Burton Ale (1036) from Rayment of Hertfordshire, a subsidiary of Greene King.

BBB Arkell's Best Bitter Beer (1038) from Swindon. The ordinary cask bitter, John Arkell, used to be known as BB. Gales of Hampshire also brew a cask BBB (1037) – which, following repeated enquiries about what it means, the brewery have called Butser Brew Bitter after a local hill.

BBBB Berrow Brewery Best Bitter (1038) from Somerset.

Beach's Borough Cask bitter (1038) from the Market Brewery, Southwark, London.

Beamish Guinness is not the only stout in Ireland. Beamish & Crawford of Cork also produce a fine example, besides brewing Bass and Carling Black Label under licence. The brewery is owned by Carling of Canada.

Bear Ale Strong draught ale (1050) from Traquair House, Scotland. Named after the famous 'Bear Gates' at this stately home, which have been closed since 1745 after Bonnie Prince Charlie passed through.

Beard Sussex family company with 27 pubs, which stopped brewing at its Star Lane premises in the 1950s, and now takes its beers from its Lewes neighbours, Harveys, under its own name. See *Harvey*.

Beaver Greenall Whitley's oddly-named bottled export lager (1045) from the 'Cumbrian Brewery' in Warrington, Cheshire.

Beck The largest exporter of German beer, based in Bremen, widely known for its Beck's Bier, which is now imported into Britain both in bottle and keg (1045) by Scottish & Newcastle. Also brewed under licence in South Africa.

Becket Name of Alexandra Brewery's wide range of cask beers from Brighton. See *Alexandra*.

Beechwood Chiltern premium cask bitter (1043) from Buckinghamshire.

Beehive Brakspear's keg bitter (1035) from Henley-on-Thames. The busy bee is also the symbol of Boddingtons of Manchester.

Beer The generic term for a non-distilled alcoholic drink produced by fermentation of a wort derived from mashed grain.

Beer Engine (1) The traditional method for drawing beer from the cellar. The beer engine, or handpump, is a suction pump designed to pull up a half-pint at each stroke. (2) The name of a home-brew pub near Exeter. *Cask beers*: Rail Ale (1037), Piston Bitter (1044).

Beer Garden An outdoor drinking area originally rich in floral decoration, now characterised by swings, sandpits, and sometimes games of boules.

Beermat A mat, originally made of cork and now usually of thin card, for soaking up beer spillage under glasses. Beermats are regarded by breweries as promotional material and by many customers as collectable items; the word 'tegestologist' has been coined for a collector of beermats.

Belhaven Scotland's oldest and most colourful independent brewery, situated at Dunbar on the east coast, near Edinburgh, and dating back to 1719. One of the leading British breweries in the export market, notably to America and Italy. Owned by the Virani hotel group. *Cask beers*: 60/- Light (1031), 70/- Heavy (1036), 80/- Export (1042), 90/- Strong Ale (1070). *Keg*: Similar range to cask, plus Special (1037).

Bottled: Pale Ale (1031), Stout (1033), Export or Scottish Ale (1041). Also brew Fowler's Wee Heavy (1070) for Tennents; and, purely for export to Italy: Pale Ale (1046), Winston's Stout (1053), Monkscroft House Ale (1070). To America: Texas Ale (1056).

Belle Vue A mass-marketed Belgian Gueuze beer from Brussels.

Ben Truman Watney's national keg bitter (1038) from Truman, London. The bottled Export is stronger (1045).

Bennets Strong ale (1057) from the Five Towns brewery, Stoke-on-Trent.

Benskins Ind Coope's northern Home Counties company with some 650 pubs. Named after the Watford brewery closed in 1972, with the name revived in 1980. Draught Benskins beers are brewed at Romford and bottled at Burton. *Cask beer*: Bitter (1037). *Keg*: Pale (1032). *Bottled*: Strong Ale (1053), Colne Spring (1082).

Bergman's Peter Walker's keg lager (1033) from Wrexham.

Berliner Weisse The bottle-conditioned white beer of Berlin. Brewed using wheat to a low alcohol content of about 3 per cent, this refreshing summer drink is often laced with woodruff or raspberry juice to give a violent green or red colour. The major brands are Kindl and Schultheiss.

Berrow Small Somerset brewery at Burnham-on-Sea set up in 1982, serving 20 local outlets. *Cask beers*: BBBB (1038), Topsy Turvy (1055).

Best Overused description for many milds and bitters, often where no 'ordinary' is offered. The best-known Best is probably Courage's Best Bitter (1039), claimed to be the best-selling real ale in the South.

Bevvy Slang term, especially in the north, for beer or drink. Derives from beverage.

Bière de Garde The smooth 'laying-down beer' of Northern France, which appears in wine-shaped, wire-corked bottles. The best example is Jenlain and the best-known St Leonard.

Big Ben Thwaites bottled strong ale (1050) from Blackburn.

Bigbury Cask best bitter (1044) from Summerskill, Devon.

Big Lamp Small Newcastle-upon-Tyne brewery begun in 1982. *Cask beers*: Bitter (1040), Extra Special (1052), Old Genie (1070).

Bine The climbing stem of the hop plant.

Birell The low-alcohol lager from Hurlimann of Switzerland now widely available in Britain. Unlike other near beers, Birell uses a special yeast so that only 0.8 per cent alcohol is produced.

Bishop Small brewery in Somerset set up in 1984, brewing Bishop's PA (1037) and Best Bitter (1041).

Bishop's Ale Ridley's strong draught and bottled barley wine (1080) from Essex, named after Bishop Ridley who was martyred at Oxford in 1555. The current Ridley family are direct descendants, and the Bishop's face is featured on all bottle labels.

Bishop's Finger Shepherd Neame's strong bottled ale (1053) from Kent, named after the finger signposts traditionally used in the county.

Bishop's Tipple Gibbs Mew's powerful cask and bottled barley wine (1066) from Salisbury, which would soon have most clerics on their knees.

Bitter A generic term for highly hopped ales, ranging from 1030 to around 1055 OG; within this range, the term is most commonly applied to 'drinking bitters' in the 1032-1044 OG band. The commonest type of draught ale, low in carbonation; best served at about 13°C (55°F).

Bitter Ale Popular name for low-gravity bitters, particularly in the southwest and South Wales, such as Courage's cask Bitter Ale (1030) from Bristol.

Blackamoor Hardys & Hansons bottled sweet stout (1044) from Nottingham.

Black and Tan Stout mixed half and half with bitter or mild.

Blackawton Devon's oldest brewery – dating back to 1977! One of the pioneers of the new brewery movement, serving 55 outlets around Totnes. *Cask beers*: Blackawton Bitter (1037), Squires (1044). *Keg and bottle*: Devon Best (1036).

Black Beer A syrupy bottled malt extract chiefly produced by Mathers of Leeds, with 7 per cent alcohol. Usually mixed with lemonade to make 'Sheffield Stout' or with rum to make the original, lethal 'rum and black'.

Black Bess Timothy Taylor's bottled stout (1043) from Yorkshire, with Dick Turpin riding across the label.

Black Bull Theakston's keg bitter (1035), named after the North Yorkshire brewers' old black bull symbol.

Black Country Holden's cask bitter (1039) and Simpkiss bottled old ale (1052) from the West Midlands.

Black Horse Godson's premium cask bitter (1048), popularly known in East London as GBH.

Black Malt Specially malted barley achieved by roasting kiln-dried malt. Used mainly for adding colour to beer as it has a low potential extract value.

Blackpool Best Rare strong cask mild (1036) from Bass, found in northwest England.

Black Prince Crown Brewery's keg dark mild (1036) from South Wales.

Black Velvet Stout and champagne. The poor man's version is stout and cider.

Blanket Pressure A low pressure of carbon dioxide applied to beer in the cask to prevent its exposure to air. Not liked by CAMRA because of the difficulty of controlling the amount of gas taken up by the beer, so making it 'fizzy'.

Blitz-Weinhard The brewers of the strongest United States beer, Olde English 800 (7.5 per cent alcohol), from Portland, Oregon. The brewery is also known for its premium lager, Henry Weinhard's Private Reserve.

Blue Popular name for Canada's best-selling lager from Labatt, and Ruddles 'ordinary' Rutland Bitter (1032) from Rutland.

Blue Anchor Ancient thatched home-brew pub in the centre of Helston, Cornwall, with powerful ales from another age. *Cask beers*: Mild (1040), Medium (1050), BB (1053), Special (1066), Extra Special (1070).

Blue Label Bottled beers from Harveys of Sussex (1038) and Timothy Taylor of West Yorkshire (1043).

Blue Star The sign of Newcastle Breweries beers.

Blue Triangle Bass's bottled pale ale (1041). Red Triangle used to indicate that it was a sediment beer – now called Worthington White Shield.

Bobby Ales Beers from Randall of Guernsey.

Bock The name of a strong German lager style, originating in Einbeck, Lower Saxony, but now more associated with Munich. Dark and pale types are produced with an alcohol content of at least 6 per cent. The beer is often linked with seasonal festivals, particularly in autumn or May (Maibock). Bock also means billy goat, and a goat's head often features on the label. In a typical act of European unity, Bock (or Bok) in France and Belgium means a beer of low strength. See also *Doppelbock* and *Eisbock*.

Boddingtons Manchester's best-known brewery, next to Strangeways prison. 'Boddys' famously fought off Allied Breweries' takeover attempt in 1970 – and then swallowed Oldham Brewery. All 281 pubs serve real ale, but the popular straw-coloured bitter has lost its distinctive character. *Cask beers*: Mild (1033), Bitter (1035), which are also bottled and canned (Bodkan).

Bodicote Small brewery at the Plough, Bodicote, Banbury, Oxon. *Cask beers*: Jim's Brew (1036), No 9 (1043).

Boil The step in the brewing process where the wort is boiled with the hops in the copper is conventionally known as 'the Boil'.

Bombardier Premium cask bitter (1042) from Charles Wells of Bedford, named after boxer Bombardier Billy Wells, the man who used to wield the Rank gong at the cinema. Also bottled for export at 1046.

Boozer Slang term for either a noted drinker or a pub.

Border The last independent brewery in North Wales – taken over and the Wrexham brewery closed down by Marstons in 1984. Now all 'Border' beers are brewed at Burton for the 170 pubs. *Cask beers*: 4X Mild (1030), Exhibition (1034), Bitter (1034). *Keg*: As cask, plus Marcher Lager (1034). See *Marstons*.

Border Scotch Theakston's keg beer (1035) brewed for the northeast.

Borough Brown Shepherd Neame's bottled brown ale (1034) from Faversham, Kent.

Borve House Britain's most northerly brewery, on the Isle of Lewis. *Cask beers*: Pale Ale (1038), Heavy (1043), Extra (1085).

Bosham Small West Sussex brewery set up in Bosham in 1984. *Cask beers*: Old Bosham (1044), FSB (1058).

Bosun Premium bitter (1048) from the Brewhouse, Poole, Dorset. Also Southsea's cask dark mild (1032) from Portsmouth.

Botanical Beer Non-alcoholic brews produced in the days of the Temperance Movement, especially popular in areas where that movement was strong, such as Birmingham. Old stone jars from 'Botanical' breweries are commonly found among pub bric-a-brac.

Bottle-conditioned A bottled beer in which a secondary fermentation takes place in the bottle. Such beers have a sediment and must be stored and served with care. Nationally known examples are Guinness and White Shield Worthington.

Bottom Fermentation Fermentation in which the yeast cells sink to the bottom of the vessel. This is a property of certain yeast strains, in particular those such as *Saccharomyces uvarum* (formerly *S. carlsbergensis*), used for lager production. Bottom fermentation is usally conducted at low temperature, $10°C$ ($50°F$) or below, thus being considerably slower than *top fermentation*. These yeasts form less of a head than *S. cerevisiae*, the top-fermenting ale yeasts. Nearly all wine is also produced with bottom-fermenting yeasts.

Bottoms The sediment left at the bottom of the cask – contains yeast and finings and any hops that have been added to the cask. Also known as *lees*.

Bourne Valley Small Hampshire brewery set up in 1978 in Andover by a former CAMRA national chairman. Owns one pub. *Cask beers*: Weaver's Bitter (1037), Andover Ale (1040), Henchard Bitter (1045), Wallop (1056).

Bowman Charles Wells bottled brown ale (1030). The Bedford brewers also use the name for their exported strong ale (1054).

Brains 'It's Brains you want' is still the cry around Cardiff, where this independent Welsh brewery serves excellent real ales in all 120 pubs. *Cask beers*: Red Dragon or RD Dark (1035), Bitter (1035.3), SA (1042). *Keg*: Capi- tal (1033). *Bottled*: Brown Ale (1033), Light Ale (1033), Extra Stout (1037), IPA (1046). Also in 2-pint flagons: Dark Mild (1033), Bitter Ale (1033). About to brew lager.

Brakspear Traditional family brewery in Henley-on-Thames, Oxfordshire, since 1779, with 122 largely unspoilt pubs selling a fine range of *cask beers*: XXX Mild (1030), Bitter or Pale Ale (1035), Special (1043), XXXX Old (1043). *Keg*: KPA or Beehive (1035).

Brau AG The brewing giant of Austria, based in Linz, which also owns the Schwechat brewery near Vienna where Anton Dreher produced the first bottom-fermenting lager beer in 1841.

Braye The only brewery on Alderney in the Channel Islands, set up in 1984 brewing malt-extract Alderney Ale (1035).

Breaker Bass's bottled malt liquor (1047) from Tennents.

Breathalyser A device to enable police to gauge the alcohol consumption of a motor-vehicle driver. Has led to a reduction in motor accidents, and a decline in trade for rural pubs.

Brenin Crown Brewery's light keg bitter (1034) from South Wales.

Brew XI Mitchells & Butlers cask and keg bitter (1040) from Birmingham.

Breweriana A manufactured word to describe ephemera, collectable bits and pieces deriving from breweries or pubs. Breweriana include beermats and other point-of-sale advertising devices, beer bottle labels, ashtrays etc, and obviously items are worth more if the products or companies they advertise are now defunct. Auctions of breweriana have been known to raise four-figure sums.

Brewers Bitter Ind Coope Romford Brewery's cask bitter (1037) for its own 75 pubs.

Brewer's Choice The premium top-fermented ale (1050) from Farsons of Malta.

Brewers' Droop Slang term for a man's inability to copulate owing to having drunk too much alcohol.

Brewers Gold Truman's bottled strong ale (1078) from London.

Brewers' Tudor An architectural style favoured for suburban pubs in the early 20th century, with gables and exposed timbers, imitative of manor houses. Often clumsily carried out, and derisorily referred to as Tudorbethan.

Brewery-conditioned Beer which has completed all its conditioning in the brewery, and then been filtered and (usually) pasteurised, ie tank or keg beer.

Brewery Tap Town breweries almost always had a pub built into the premises – the 'Brewery Tap'. Otherwise the nearest pub to a brewery, hopefully patronised by brewery workers who know a good pint. If they're all in a rival brewer's pub – beware!

Brewex Britain's brewing trade fair held every few years. Best known for its beer championships, in which most British breweries compete for medals.

Brewhouse The business part of a brewery, where the beer is produced. Also the name of a home-brew pub owned by Poole Brewery in Poole High Street, Dorset. *Cask beers*: High Street Mild (1035), Bitter (1036), Bosun (1048), Dave's Lager (1048).

Brewhouse Ale Premium bitter (1055) from Reepham Brewery, Norfolk.

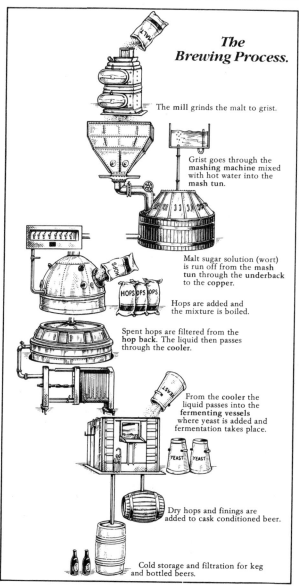

The Brewing Process.

The mill grinds the malt to grist.

Grist goes through the **mashing machine** mixed with hot water into the **mash tun.**

Malt sugar solution (wort) is run off from the mash tun through the **underback** to the copper.

Hops are added and the mixture is boiled.

Spent hops are filtered from the **hop back.** The liquid then passes through the **cooler.**

From the cooler the liquid passes into the **fermenting vessels** where yeast is added and fermentation takes place.

Dry hops and finings are added to cask conditioned beer.

Cold storage and filtration for keg and bottled beers.

Reproduced by permission of Eldridge Pope & Co., brewers of Huntsman Ales in Dorchester.

Brewmaster Whitbread's bottled export ale (1042).

Brewster Centuries-old term for a lady brewer; also sometimes used for a male brewer, or a brewer of either sex.

Brewster Sessions The annual licensing court which deals especially with licence renewals and amendments to permitted hours. Sessions begin in early February each year. Licences are usually granted en bloc.

Brew Ten Bass keg bitter (1036) in the north.

Bridge Cask bitter (1042) from Burton Bridge, Burton-upon-Trent.

Bridge House Home-brew pub next to Tower Bridge, London. *Cask beers*: Bermondsey (1036), Special (1048), 007 (1055).

Bridgewater Arms Home-brew pub at Little Gaddesden, Herts, expanding into the free trade. *Cask beers*: Best (1035), Earl's Bitter (1048), Old Santa (1066).

Bright Beer A term often used for chilled and filtered beers.

Bristol Hall's small real ale brewery at their Nailsea depot near Bristol, producing Jacobs Best (1038) and Bristol Pride (1045).

Broadside Adnams strong, bottled pale ale (1068) from Suffolk, named after the battle of Sole Bay in 1672.

Brock Aptly-named lager (1033) from Hall & Woodhouse, the 'Badger' brewers of Dorset.

Broughton One of the most successful of the new breweries in Britain, set up in the Scottish Borders near Biggar in 1980 and now serving over 200 outlets. *Cask beer*: Greenmantle Ale (1038). *Keg*: Broughton Ale (1036). *Bottled*: Greenmantle (1038), Old Jock (1070).

Brown One of the northwest's major brewers, with 550 pubs, Matthew Brown are popularly known as 'Lion Ales'. In 1984 this Blackburn company took over the much smaller but more famous Yorkshire brewers, Theakston, giving the group a total of four breweries at Blackburn, Masham, Carlisle, and Workington. *Cask beers*: Lion Mild (1031), Lion Bitter (1036), John Peel (1040). *Keg*: Same range as cask, plus Matty's Light (1033), Slalom Lager (1036), Slalom D (1045). *Bottled*:

Original Brown (1032), Light Ale (1033), Export IPA (1038) – known as Crystal in pint bottles – King's Ale (1060), Slalom (1036), Slalom D (1045), Slalom International (1068). See also *Theakston*.

Brown Ale Commonly a bottled, sweetish mild ale; usually dark, low in alcohol, and very lightly hopped. There are exceptions (eg Newcastle Brown Ale and Sam Smith's Strong Brown Ale) which are of higher gravity and flavour, but are still sweet rather than bitter.

Brown Bracer Crown Brewery's bottled brown ale (1033) from South Wales.

Brown Oxford Morrell's bottled brown ale (1032) from Oxford.

Brown Peter Peter Walker's bottled brown ale (1034) from Warrington.

Brown Stout Holt's bottled stout (1040) from Manchester.

Bruce Chain of seven home-brew pubs in London, under the 'Firkin' banner.

Brummie Davenport's bottled brown ale (1032) from, of course, Birmingham.

Buckley Wales's oldest brewery, in the rugby stronghold of Llanelli, with 180 pubs. Has a major stake in its close neighbours, Felinfoel, while Whitbread has a major stake in Buckley! *Cask beers*: Standard Bitter (1032), Mild (1032), Best Bitter (1036). *Keg*: Same range as cask, plus Celtic Bright (1033) and Gold (1043). *Bottled*: Bitter Ale (1032), Brown Ale (1032), Gold (1043).

Budvar The original and best Budweiser, claim the Czechs; the well-known American beer takes its name from Budvar's home town of Ceske Budejovice (Budweis in German), which was supplying the Bohemian court with beer in the 16th century. American 'Bud' is lagered for a minimum of three weeks; Budvar say their 'original' is conditioned for over three months. The Czech beer is also stronger.

Budweiser The world's best-selling beer, from Anheuser-Busch of St Louis, launched in 1876 as the first American national brand. It takes its name from the Czechoslovakian town of Ceske Budejovice (Budweis in German), and is brewed with rice as well as malted barley, and fined over beechwood chips. 'Bud' (1044) is now also brewed under licence by Watneys in England.

Buff's Strong cask bitter (1050) from Canterbury Brewery, Kent.

Bullards Norwich old ale (1057), named after one of the local breweries taken over and closed down by Watneys. Christmas brew in polypins.

Bulldog Courage's specially-conditioned, bottled pale ale (1068), produced in agreement with London beer distributors, Robert Porter, whose symbol is the bulldog.

Bulls Eye Greenall Whitley bottled brown ale (1035) from Warrington.

Bunce Small Wiltshire brewery at Netheravon, set up in 1984. *Cask beer*: Bunce's Best (1043).

Bunghole The aperture through which a cask is filled with beer before being closed by the shive.

Burkes Small brewery at the Lion pub, Croydon, also serving the Hole in the Wall, Waterloo. *Cask beers*: Original (1034), Best Bitter (1042).

Burke's Irish Brigade Another 'Irish joke' beer. This bottled stout is in fact produced in England by Greenall Whitley of Warrington for export.

Burns Drybrough's keg special (1036) from Edinburgh, named after the famous poet. Canned as Burns's Scottish Ale.

Burslem Ansell's subsidiary company in the Potteries, serving some 350 pubs with Tetley as well as Ansell's beers.

Bursley Cask bitter (1040) from Five Towns brewery, Stoke-on-Trent.

Burt The only Isle of Wight brewery, at Ventnor, serving the best-value beers in the South of England in its 11 pubs. *Cask beers*: LB (1030), Dark Mild (1030), VPA (1040), 4X (1040). *Bottled*:

Pale Ale (1030), Nut Brown (1030), Golden IPA (1040), 4X Strong Brown (1040).

Burton Ale Once a general name for beers brewed at Burton-upon-Trent, England's capital of brewing, where the well water, with its high concentration of calcium and magnesium salts, makes it ideal for brewing strong pale ales. Since 1976, name chiefly used for Ind Coope's premium cask bitter (1047.5). Also Greene King bottled ale (1031).

Burton Bitter Marston's cask and keg bitter (1037) from Burton-upon-Trent.

Burton Brewery Allied's major brewery at Burton-upon-Trent, capable of brewing 2.5 million barrels a year. Also runs some 40 pubs around Burton. See *Ind Coope*.

Burton Bridge Small brewery set up in England's brewing capital, Burton-upon-Trent, in 1982, serving some 40 outlets including its own bar at the brewery. *Cask beers*: Bridge Bitter (1042), Burton Porter (1045), Festival Ale (1055), Old Expensive (1065). *Bottled*: Burton Porter (1045), plus a wide variety of special brews.

Burtonise One of the main factors that made Burton-upon-Trent such an important brewing centre was the quality of the local well water. This contains a range of salts, most especially gypsum (calcium sulphate), that are perfect for producing pale ales and bitter beers. So acclaimed is the Burton water that now many brewers add chemicals to their brewing liquor (water) to make its composition identical to Burton; this process is Burtonising.

Burton Mild Everards mild (1033) from their Burton brewery which is now run by a trust as a national brewery museum.

Burton Porter Dark cask ale (1045) from Burton Bridge. Also bottle-conditioned.

Burton Union A fermentation method, unique to Burton-upon-Trent, during which the beer rises out of large oak casks through swan-neck pipes into long troughs for use in pitching into following brews. It is this system which made Draught Bass famous, but they closed their Union rooms in the early 1980s, and now only Marstons retain this quality method of brewing for their Pedigree ale.

Burtonwood Regional brewery near Warrington, under the Forshaw family, owning 290 scattered pubs including many in North Wales. *Cask beers*: Dark Mild (1032), Best Bitter (1036.5), Almond's Best Bitter (1036.5). *Bottled*: Super Brown Ale (1032), Krystal Lite (1030), Special Pale Ale (1037), Top Hat (1046). The last three are also kegged, as are the mild and bitter.

Bush Beer Despite its English name, this is an unusual Belgian strong ale, containing a potent 9.5 per cent alcohol.

Butcombe One of the most successful of the new breweries, set up in the Mendip Hills near Bristol in 1978 by a former managing director of Courage Western. Now selling over 120 barrels a week of one cask beer: Butcombe Bitter (1039).

Butt A huge cask of 108 gallons, no longer used for beer. The wine trade, however, still uses the name for large casks of a variety of sizes.

BVA Winkle's Birch Vale Ale (1037), from North Derbyshire, often sold under 'house' names.

BYB Bentley's Yorkshire Bitter – Whitbread's weak keg (1033) from Sheffield, named after Bentley's brewery in Woodlesford, closed in 1972.

[C]

Caledonian Lorimer & Clark's rich strong ale (1077) from the Caledonian Brewery in Edinburgh.

Cambrian Ansell's subsidiary company in South Wales, with 174 pubs. Has its own cask Dark (1034) specially brewed in Wales.

Cambridge Paine's bottled pale ale (1052) from St Neots, produced for export.

Cameron The northeast's major brewers of real ale, notably Strongarm. But recently the Hartlepool brewery with 500 pubs has faced an uncertain future following the takeover of its parent group, Ellerman Lines. In 1984 its sale to Scottish & Newcastle Breweries was stopped only by the intervention of the Monopolies Commission. *Cask beers*: Lion Bitter (1036), Strongarm (1040). *Keg*: As cask, plus Mild (1032), Light (1032), Crown (1040), Hansa (1036). *Bottled*: Brown Ale (1032), Light Ale (1036), Strongarm Special (1046).

Campbells Very strong bottled 'Scotch' and 'Christmas' ales brewed by Whitbread – for sale to the Belgians. The name comes from Campbell, Hope & King, the beloved Edinburgh brewery cynically taken over by Whitbread in 1967 and closed in 1971.

CAMRA The Campaign for Real Ale began in 1971 as a reaction against bland keg beers foisted on the public by the national brewers, who dominated Britain and threatened to crush the remaining independent companies. So successful was the Campaign that not only did traditional brewers flourish as interest in their beer soared, but the 'Big Six' were forced to brew real ale again. Today CAMRA's 18,000 members are involved not only in fighting for real choice in every bar, but also in opposing brewery takeovers, pub closures, restrictive licensing hours, soaring beer prices, etc. CAMRA is the only voice of the drinker in an industry still dominated by national combines.

Canterbury The first of the new breweries in Kent, set up in 1979, which since 1983 has had its beer brewed under contract by Tisbury. *Cask beers*: Canterbury Ale (1038), Buff's Bitter (1050). *Bottled*: Canterbury Premium (1039).

Cantillon Unusual Belgian museum brewery in Anderlecht, Brussels, producing wild Lambic beers, which accepts visitors in the summer.

Capital Marston's cask light mild (1030) from Burton-upon-Trent and, more appropriately, Brain's keg (1033) from the Welsh capital.

Captain's Southsea's cask bitter (1037) from Portsmouth.

Caramel Brown roasted sugar used to add colour and sweetness to dark beers.

Carapils or **caramalt** Lightly kilned malt used for lager brewing.

Carbohydrate Sugars and starches from the malt are the main carbohydrates in beer. The more the beer is attenuated, the lower the residual carbohydrate level. Such 'dry' beers can be suitable for some diabetics, although the high calorie content makes them useless for weight control.

Carbonation The addition of carbon dioxide to bottled beer or soft drinks to produce a fizzy drink.

Carbon Dioxide (CO_2) One of the waste products produced by the yeast as it consumes the sugars in the wort (another is alcohol). Much of the carbon dioxide is given off from the fermenting vessels (big breweries often sell it as a by-product), but much remains dissolved in the beer. This is essential to give the beer its condition. The amount of CO_2 that enters the beer depends upon the beer temperature and the CO_2 pressure; cooling the beer or increasing the pressure will increase the amount dissolved.

Carling Black Label The ubiquitous lager brewed under licence from Carling O'Keefe of Toronto in many countries, including Britain, where it is brewed by Bass. In Britain Carling (1037) is the bland leader, followed by Skol, Heineken, and Carlsberg.

Carling O'Keefe The Canadian brewery whose former owner, Eddie Taylor, helped create the Bass Charrington giant in Britain through a series of brewery takeovers in the 1960s – to gain outlets for his Black Label lager. Carling also own Beamish in Eire and are now part of the South African Rupert group.

Carlsberg The famous Danish brewers who perfected the bottom-fermenting yeast, *Saccharomyces carlsbergensis*, now used by lager brewers everywhere. Their beers are brewed around the globe, either under licence or by local companies. The British brewery at Northampton produces 'probably the weakest lager in the world' in Carlsberg Pilsner (1030), its premium Hof (1042) being the standard Danish Carlsberg, with the bottled Export (1048) the international strength. In contrast, Carlsberg Special (1080) is probably the strongest lager brewed in Britain.

Carlton United The giant of the Australian brewing industry, best known in its Melbourne home for its Carlton and Victoria beers, but outside Australia famed for its 'tubes' of Fosters. A weaker beer under this name is now produced by Watneys in Britain.

Carr's See *Gate.*

Cascade The chief American variety of hop. Cascade is also the name of Tasmania's main brewery.

Cask The general name for the containers used for traditional draught beer. See *Piggin, Pin, Firkin, Kilderkin, Barrel,* and *Hogshead.*

Cask Breather A device that allows the beer drawn from a cask to be replaced by CO_2 at atmospheric pressure. The cask breather is used to maintain the condition of beers that have to remain in cask for more than a few days. Also known as a *demand valve* or *aspirating valve.*

Cask-Condition The quintessence of Real Ale – the beer put into the cask must contain enough yeast for a slow secondary fermentation to take place. This fermentation produces the subtle matured flavours that distinguish Real Ale from dead 'keg' beers.

Castle Jennings of Cumbria keg mild (1033) and bitter (1035). Also bottled special pale ales from Morrell of Oxford (1041) and McMullen of Hertford (1047).

Castle Eden Whitbread's County Durham brewery whose Castle Eden Ale is now sold throughout the country. *Cask beers*: Durham Ale (1036), Castle Eden (1041). *Keg*: Whitbread Ordinary (1033), Best Scotch (1035), Trophy Special (1040).

Castlemaine XXXX Allied Breweries has jumped on the 'Australian' lager bandwagon by launching Castlemaine-Tooheys leading brand in Britain. But Allied's keg 'Four-Ex' (1035) is brewed in Wrexham to a weaker recipe. The canned version (1043) is imported.

Castlemaine-Tooheys Two of Australia's best-known

brewers, Castlemaine of Brisbane and Tooheys of Sydney, merged in 1980 to challenge the might of Carlton United (CUB). Partly owned by Allied Breweries of Britain.

Castletown The smaller of the Isle of Man's two breweries, serving excellent 'Ale of Man' under the island's Pure Beer Act (only malt, hops, and sugar) for its 35 pubs. Once produced the famous Oyster Stout – with real oysters. *Cask beers*: Mild (1036), Bitter (1036). *Bottled*: Nut Brown (1036), Red Seal (1036), Liqueur Barley Wine (1072).

CB Cadnam Bitter – New Forest weak keg (1031) from Hampshire.

Celebrated Oatmeal Stout Sam Smith's bottled strong stout (1050) for export.

Celebration Morrell's strong cask and bottled brew (1066) from Oxford.

Cellar A room in a pub where the beer casks are stored. Traditionally below ground to keep a steady low temperature, but the modern cellar is now often at street level and air-conditioned. 13°C (about 55°F) is the ideal cellar temperature.

Cellar Brewery See *Cirencester*.

Celtic Bright Buckley's low-gravity keg and canned bitter (1033) from Llanelli, South Wales.

Celtic Gold Silverthorne's cask lager (1046) from South Wales.

Centenary Strong bottled ales brewed by Mitchells of Lancaster (1080) and Home of Nottingham (1060) to celebrate their first 100 years in 1980 and 1978 respectively. And still going strong today.

Centrifuge A filter vessel in which the beer is made to spin rapidly: heavy sediments collect at the outside and lighter material at the centre. Often known as a *whirlpool*.

Chairman's Choice Alternative name for Gibbs Mew's Anchor Keg (1039) from Salisbury.

Challenger Cask bitter (1039) from Ashford Brewery, Kent.

Champion Bottled pale ales from Adnams (1032), Gales (1040), and Greenall Whitley (1038).

Charger Tennent's weak canned lager (1032) from Scotland.

Charles Wells See *Wells.*

Charrington After merging with Bass in 1967, London's famous Toby brewers lost their brewery, and now 'the best-selling real ale around London,' Charrington IPA (1039), is brewed in Wolverhampton. Other Charrington brands include keg Light Mild (1033), bottled Prize Medal (1035), and Barley Wine (1064). Runs 1500 pubs in the southeast. See also *Toby.*

Chequer Davenport's keg (1036.5) and bottled (1032) bitter from Birmingham.

Cherrys Part of the Guinness-controlled Irish Ale Breweries, in Waterford.

Cheshire English Pub Beer This bottled mouthful (1045) from Greenall Whitley of Warrington, produced for export to America, qualifies as the corniest beer name.

Chesters Whitbread's Manchester trading company and Salford brewery with two local cask and keg beers: Best Mild (1033), Best Bitter (1034) – sold as Duttons further north. Also keg Chester's Light (1032).

Chester Brown See *Old Chester.*

Chester Gold See *Old Glory.*

Chestnut John Smith's dark keg mild (1033) from Tadcaster.

Chill (1) '*Chilled and filtered*' is a common description for brewery-conditioned bright beer. The beer is cooled, almost to freezing, which causes the suspended proteins to separate out; they can then be filtered off to leave a clear product. **(2)** *Chill haze*: if a cask-conditioned beer is allowed to get too cold, the protein separation will produce a cloudiness that will not settle out. Whilst spoiling the appearance of the beer, it makes no appreciable difference to the flavour.

Chiltern Small Buckinghamshire brewery near Aylesbury, started in

1980, now supplying some British Rail mainline stations in London. *Cask beers*: Chiltern Ale (1036), Beechwood Bitter (1043).

Chimay The classic Belgian Trappist ales produced by the Abbaye of Chimay on the French border. The three famous bottle-conditioned beers – Capsule Rouge (6.6 per cent alcohol), Blanche (7.5), and Bleu (8.5) – are distinguished by the colour of their bottle tops. The blue is even vintage-dated, reaching its peak after two years.

Chiswick Fuller's cask bitter (1035.5) from London.

Chocks Wooden blocks used to secure casks while on stillage.

Chocolate Malt Specially malted barley treated in the same fashion as black malt, without as high a kilning temperature.

Christmas Ales Rich festive ales, often available in polypins, are brewed by a number of British brewers. McMullen of Hertford (1070) and Greene King of East Anglia (1052) actually call theirs Christmas Ale – though the Greene King name, surprisingly, comes from the Suffolk brewery of F.C. Christmas, taken over in 1918. Strong, bottled Christmas Ales are also a Belgian speciality. Shepherd Neame of Kent produce a notable English example (1068), as do Harveys of Sussex (1090).

Christmas Cracker Wood's dark winter brew (1060) from Shropshire.

Christmas Reserve Mauldon's powerful festive brew (1065) from Suffolk; available in December only.

Chudley See *Godson Chudley*.

Cirencester Small brewery, also known as the Cellar Brewery, set up in Cirencester, Gloucestershire, in 1983. *Cask beers*: Cirencester Bitter (1036), Best Bitter (1040), Down Moore Ale (1042), Abbey Ale (1047).

Cisk The award-winning lager (1042) from Malta's only brewery, Farsons, which is better known for its ales.

Clarifier See *Anchor Steam*.

Clark Yorkshire beer wholesalers who began brewing again in 1982. The stronger ales are brewed chiefly for their

Henry Boon pub alongside the Wakefield brewery and depot. *Cask beers*: Traditional Bitter (1038.5), Henry Boon's Wakefield Ale (1038.5), Hammerhead (1050), XS (1052).

Clausthaler Low-alcohol (0.6 per cent) bottled lager imported from Germany.

Clayson Report The government report on the Scottish licensing law made in 1976, headed by Dr Christopher Clayson. It led to the passing of the 1976 Licensing (Scotland) Act, which allows pubs to apply for regular extensions to permitted hours and so remain open all day in Scotland. See *Scottish Hours*.

Clifton Inns Watney-associated company running 120 traditional pubs, including five home-brew pubs.

Closing Time The dreaded moment when the publican is required to have you leave his premises. This is usually straight after drinking-up time, averaging ten minutes after official last orders have been served.

Club Room A disappearing facility – a private room where folk clubs, pigeon societies, angling clubs, and even CAMRA branches can meet and drink while pursuing their hobby or business without disturbing regular customers.

Coaching Inn An old hostelry once used as a regular picking up and setting down point for horse-drawn coach passengers, usually offering accommodation, food, and stabling for replacement horses. Often characterised by arched entry passages leading to a rear yard.

Coaster Another name for *Beermat*.

Cock Robin Robinson's keg bitter (1035) from Stockport.

Coigns A Scottish term for *Chocks*.

Collar The space between the tops or measure line of a glass and the beer surface. Usually used deprecatingly as '. . . could you top-up the collar please . . .'.

College Many colleges at Oxford and Cambridge used to brew their own special ales; the last, at The Queen's College, Oxford, stopped in 1939. This cask and bottled brew from Morrell of Oxford (1073) reflects that tradition.

Colne Spring Benskins famous strong bottled ale from Watford, which the new Ind Coope company has revived as a winter drink (1082), though now brewed at Burton and no longer a sediment beer.

Colt 45 Courage's canned malt liquor (1047).

Combes Watney's cask bitter (1041), named after the London brewery which amalgamated with Watneys in 1898.

Condition To be palatable, beer must contain dissolved carbon dioxide; this gives it freshness and sharpens the flavour. The amount of dissolved gas is known as the 'condition'. Too much condition leads to frothiness and over-sharp flavours (as with keg beers); too little condition makes the beer flat and insipid. Maintaining the correct condition is a skilled job.

Conical (Fermenter) A modern type of fermenting vessel in the shape of a tall cylinder with a tapered lower end. Injected air keeps the fermenting mixture agitated. Many believe that conical fermentation vessels do not produce the same flavours as the more traditional systems but this must be considered 'not proven', although there is wide agreement that Draught Bass, which changed from Burton Union fermentation to conical fermentation recently, has changed in flavour.

Conqueror Powerful cask ale from Axe Vale brewery, Devon, with a gravity of 1066, of course.

Container Beer Another term for *keg* or *bright beer*.

Continental Davenport's keg and bottled lager (1034) from Birmingham.

Continuous Fermentation A modern process in which wort is passed continuously through a concentration of yeast, instead of being fermented in batches.

Cook Small brewery in Halstead, Essex, which stopped brewing in 1974, but still supplies its off-licences with bottled beers under its own label, brewed by Ridleys. *Bottled beers*: Nut Brown (1030), Golden Ale (1030), Country Brew (1050).

Cooper A maker or repairer of casks, normally only applied in the context of traditional wooden casks.

Coopers To beer connoisseurs this is *the* Australian

brewery, based in Adelaide, producing two remarkable bottle-conditioned ales fermented in wooden casks: Sparkling Ale (5.3 per cent alcohol) and Extra Stout (6.9). These are Australia's real ales.

Coors The largest single brewing plant in the world, situated in Golden, Colorado, which gained a rather folksy image for its lager because of its isolated position in the Rocky Mountains. Also brews Irish Red Ale under licence from Letts of Eire.

Copper The brewery vessel in which the wort and the hops are boiled, producing the hopped wort that will then go into the fermenting vessels. A modern copper is a closed stainless steel tank, heated by internal steam coils although, as the name suggests, these vessels were formerly made of copper. A few breweries still use open coppers with direct firing – no more than huge saucepans!

Copper Syrup See *Malt Syrup*.

Coref Ertach Pensans Penzance Heritage Fortnight special brew (1055), from Pensans Brewery, Cornwall.

Cornish Devenish cask best bitter (1042) from Redruth, Cornwall. Also canned.

Cotleigh Small brewery set up in Devon in 1979 before moving to the former Hancock's brewery, Wiveliscombe, Somerset. *Cask beers*: WB Bitter (1037), Tawny Bitter (1040), Old Buzzard (1048).

Country (**1**) McMullen's fine cask best bitter (1041) from Hertford. (**2**) Usher's keg bitter (1036) from Wiltshire.

Country Brew Cook's bottled strong pale ale (1050) brewed by Ridleys of Essex.

County Ruddles famous strong ale (1050), the only cask beer to win the Brewex supreme championship twice, in 1952 and 1980. Now increasingly sold by other brewers like Watneys.

Courage Part of the Imperial food and tobacco group since 1972, with 5,000 pubs and just three breweries at Reading, Bristol, and Tadcaster, Yorkshire (John Smith), following recent closures in London, Plymouth, and Newark. All Courage's real ale is brewed in Bristol, with the new Berkshire plant on the M4 manufacturing keg and lager. *Cask beers*: Bitter Ale (1030), Best Bitter (1039), Directors (1046). *Keg*: Simonds (1032), Dark Mild (1033), Best (1039), John Courage (1042), Harp (1032), Hofmeister (1036), Kronenbourg 1664 (1046). *Bottled*: Light (1032), Brown (1032), Velvet Stout (1042), John Courage (1042), George's Home-Brewed (1042), Bulldog (1068), Russian Stout (1100). *Canned only*: Bitter (1036), Colt 45 (1047). See also *John Smith*.

Crabbers' Nip One of Britain's best beer names, used by Devenish for their sharp barley wine (1066) in nip-size bottles, sadly now discontinued 'though it may come back'.

Cream Ale An odd American brew in which a small amount of top-fermented beer is blended with lager. The main producers are Genesee of Rochester, New York.

Cream Label Watney's bottled stout (1038).

Cream Stout Once-popular name for smoother 'milk stouts', still retained by Felinfoel of South Wales for their bottled export stout (1040).

Creedy Valley Small brewery in Crediton, Devon, set up in 1984. *Cask beers*: Creedy Bitter (1036), Tun Bitter (1041).

Cromwell Cask bitter (1037) from Marston Moor near York.

Crouch Vale Small Essex brewery set up in 1981 near Chelmsford. *Cask beers*: Woodham Bitter (1035.5), Best Bitter (1039), SAS (1048).

Crown Cameron's stronger keg bitter (1040) from Hartlepool, and Greene King's bottled pale ale (1039) from East Anglia. Also Crown Brewery beers; see below.

Crown Brewery Former United Clubs Brewery at Pontyclun, Mid Glamorgan, which changed its name to Crown in 1977, but still serves the clubs of South Wales while now owning a handful of pubs. *Cask beers*: 4X (1036), SBB (1036). *Keg*: Crown (1033), Brenin (1034), Black Prince (1036), Special (1036), Great Western (1041). *Bottled*: Amber (1033), Special (1033), Brown

Bracer (1033).

Crown Cork Metal bottle top which replaced the stopper in beer bottles.

Crown Point Home-brew cask bitter (1038) of the Crown Point Inn, Seal Chart, Kent. See *Sevenoaks*.

Crystal Eldridge Pope's keg (1034) and bottled (1030) light ale from Dorset. Also the name given to Matthew Brown's Export IPA from Blackburn in pint bottles.

Crystal Malt Barley malt primarily for ale brewing, that is removed from a standard kiln and placed into another pre-heated kiln at a higher temperature. This process produces a glossy finish to the corn, which, when used in brewing, enhances body in beer.

Curing See *Kilning*.

[D]

DAB The largest German brewery, Dortmunder Actien also owns Hansa in the same city. Best known for its dry Export and Meister Pils. Not to be confused with DUB, Dortmunder Union.

Danish Light Low-alcohol lager (less than 0.6 per cent) brewed in Copenhagen. Imported into Britain by Allied Breweries.

Danny Brown Bottled brown ale (1034) from Daniel Thwaites of Blackburn.

Dark Popular name for mild in South Wales: eg Brain's Dark.

Dark Star Pitfield's strong ale (1050), from London N1. Also naturally-conditioned in bottle.

Darley Traditional brewery with 64 pubs around Thorne in South Yorkshire, taken over in 1978 by Vaux of Sunderland, who also own Darley's neighbours, Wards of Sheffield. *Cask beers*: Mild (1033), Thorne Best Bitter (1038). *Keg*: As cask.

Dartmoor Thompson's keg bitter (1037) and lager (1036) from Ashburton, Devon.

Dash Nickname for Worthington Dark (1034) in the Swansea area.

Dashers Cask beer (1040) from the Fox & Hounds, Stottesdon, Shropshire.

Davenports Birmingham's famous 'Beer at Home' brewery specialising in bottled and canned beers, with few of its 124 scattered pubs in the city itself. Fought off a major takeover attempt by Banks's of Wolverhampton in 1983. *Cask beers*: Mild (1034.8), Bitter (1038.9). *Keg*: Mild (1034.5), Drum Bitter (1036.5), Chequer Bitter (1036.5), Continental Lager (1033.9). *Bottled*: Brummie Brown (1032), Mild Ale (1032), Chequer Bitter (1032), Best Bitter (1034), Pale Ale (1038), Stout (1038), Top Brew (1071), Top Brew De Luxe (1074), Jager Lager (1032), Continental Lager (1034).

DD See *Double Diamond*.

Decoction One of the two main methods of mashing (the other being *Infusion*). Decoction is the usual system used in Europe for lager-type beers, while infusion is the normal British system. The main difference is that while infusion takes place as a single operation at one temperature, decoction mashing is a process of several steps (usually three) with staged temperature rises, as portions of the extract are drawn off (decocted), brought to the boil, and then returned to the mash tun. The advantage claimed for this complicated system is that different enzymes are more efficient at the different temperatures so that a more complete extraction can be obtained from the lighter malts needed for lager beers.

De Koninck A fine top-fermented Belgian beer, similar to German Alt, from Antwerp's only brewery. The all-malt copper ale (5.2 per cent alcohol) is unpasteurised on draught.

Delph Strong Ale Batham's winter brew (1054) from the Delph Brewery, Brierley Hill, West Midlands. Slogan: 'Good Delph'.

De Luxe See *Top Brew*.

Demand Valve See *Cask Breather*.

Dempsey New Dublin brewery set up in 1983, introducing real ale into Eire with Dempsey's Real Ale (1037). Also produce bottled Dublin Pride (1040).

Devanha The only brewery in Northeast Scotland, set up in 1982 near Aberdeen. Named after a former Aberdeen brewery. *Cask beers*: XB (1036), XXX (1042), Pale Eighty (1042).

Devenish The major 'seaside' brewers of the southwest, with 330 pubs and two breweries in Weymouth, Dorset, and Redruth, Cornwall. The Weymouth brewery is set right in the harbour. *Cask beers*: John Devenish (1032), Wessex (1042), Cornish (1042). *Keg*: Newton's Ale (1032), Saxon (1033), John Groves (1034), Dark Mild (1035), Falmouth Bitter (1038), Grunhalle Lager (1036). *Bottled*: John Devenish (1032), Light Ale (1033), Brown Ale (1035), Wessex Pale (1042), Grunhalle DB Pils (1038). *Canned*: Cornish Best (1042).

Devizes Wadworth's light cask bitter (1030) from Wiltshire, named after their home town.

Devon Best Blackawton's filtered beer in keg and bottle (1036).

Devon Special Cask best bitter (1043) from the Mill Brewery, Newton Abbot.

Diamond Bitter Ind Coope's low gravity keg (1033) for the club trade, from Burton.

Diamond Export Bottled and canned beer (1042) from Alloa Brewery in Scotland. On draught as Alloa Export.

Diamond Heavy Keg and canned beer (1036) from Alloa Brewery.

Diät Pils These beers will not help you slim. They contain less carbohydrate as they are fermented for longer, turning the sugars to alcohol. But this means they are strong (around 6 per cent alcohol) – and alcohol is considerably more fattening than carbohydrate. They are, however, ideal for diabetics. The leading brand in Britain is Holsten from Hamburg.

Dickens Own Cask bitter (1040) for the Dickens Inn by the Tower of London, from Tooley Street Brewery. Also Special (1050).

Dinner Ale A low-gravity, usually bottled beer once made by a second mash of the malt. Recommended for consumption with meals. Now rare.

Dipstick A thin rod, usually of square section, dipped into a cask through the spile hole to measure the contents. Normally scales for four different cask sizes are engraved on the four sides.

Directors Courage's respected premium bitter (1046), rescued from obscurity by CAMRA and now widely sold throughout the south. Named after the beer the directors of Courage's former Alton brewery in Hampshire used to enjoy in the boardroom.

Dixie Well-known American brewery and beer from New Orleans, with lots of jazzy marketing.

Dog & Parrot Whitbread home-brew pub (using malt extract) in Newcastle-on-Tyne. *Cask beers*: Scotswood Ale (1036), Wallop (1046).

Dogbolter Bruce's powerful cask ale (1060) in his 'Firkin' chain of home-brew pubs, London.

Dolphin Cask best bitter (1038) and symbol of Poole Brewery, Dorset.

Dominion New Zealand's second-largest brewing group, based in Auckland, which has the doubtful distinction of having invented continuous fermentation.

Donkey Box A tiny snug capable of seating less than a dozen people.

Donnington Britain's most picturesque brewery, set in a fold of the Cotswolds near Stow-on-the-Wold, in an old stone mill by a lake. The owner of the brewery and its 17 pubs, Claude Arkell, is a relative of the Arkells of Swindon. *Cask beers*: XXX Mild (1035), BB (1035), SBA (1040). *Bottled*: Brown Ale (1035), Light Ale (1035), Double Donn (1042).

Doppelbock This extra-strong German beer style has an alcohol content of at least 7.5 per cent. The original 'double bock', produced by the Munich brewery of Paulaner, is called Salvator, and ever since the names of all Doppelbocks have ended in -*ator*, eg Optimator from Spaten and Maximator from Augustiner. See also *Eisbock*.

DORA Defence of the Realm Act, 1915. Wartime

legislation, intended only as a temporary measure, that introduced restrictions on pub opening hours for the first time, aimed at helping the war effort. The laws were consolidated in the 1921 Licensing Act, which forms the basis of current restrictions on pub hours.

Dorchester Cask bitter from Eldridge Pope (1033), named after their home town.

Dormalt Modern system of malting using a continuous conveyor.

Dorset Original IPA Eldridge Pope's cask best bitter (1041) from Dorchester.

Dortmunder Dortmund is the biggest brewing city not only in Germany but also in Europe, with a big beer style to match. Dortmunder Export is drier and stronger than lagers from Munich and Pilsen, with over 5 per cent alcohol. The best example is probably Kronen Export.

Dos Equis Surprisingly, Mexico is one of the world's major brewing nations, owing much to its Austrian Hapsburg past. Dos Equis (two crosses), a Vienna-style amber brew, is increasingly popular in the USA.

Double Brown Bateman's stronger bottled brown ale (1037) from Lincolnshire.

Double Century Younger's bottled ale (1054), first brewed to celebrate their bicentenary of brewing in Edinburgh in 1949.

Double Chance Cask bitter (1039) from Malton Brewery, North Yorkshire, named after the 1925 Grand National winner which was once stabled in the brewery buildings.

Double Dagger Strong pale ale (1050) from Oak Brewery, Cheshire.

Double Diamond Allied's faded national keg beer (1037), which was always a weak imitation of Ind Coope's Burton bottled pale ale (1043). The recipe of the original 'DD' forms the basis of cask Burton Ale.

Double Donn Donnington's bottled special bitter (1042) from the Cotswolds.

Double Dragon Felinfoel's famous premium bitter (1041) from South Wales in cask, keg, and bottle.

Double Maxim Strong bottled brown ale (1044) from

Vaux of Sunderland, originally brewed by Colonel Ernest Vaux on his return from the Boer War, and named after a machine gun.

Double Star Bottled pale ale (1040) from Charles Wells of Bedford.

Double Strong Felinfoel's bottled strong ale (1075) from South Wales, sold in America as Hercules!

Double Top Bottled brown ale (1033) from Higsons of Liverpool.

Downham Small brewery (using malt extract) at the Castle Hotel, Downham Market, Norfolk. *Cask beers*: Downham Bitter (1036), Old (1048).

Down Moore Premium cask ale (1042) from Cirencester Brewery, Glos.

Down Royal The only home-brew pub in Northern Ireland, at Lisburn, Co. Antrim. *Cask beer*: Export (1043).

DPA Mitchells & Butlers keg light mild (1033). The initials stand for Darby Pale Ale, after a West Bromwich brewery taken over by M&B in 1951.

Draught A general term for any drink that is dispensed from a bulk container into smaller measures for sale, i.e. as served over the bar from a tap in a pub. Thus Draught Beer can be either *cask-conditioned* or *brewery-conditioned*.

Draught Excluder Chudley's finely-named dark winter ale (1070) from London.

Dray A vehicle used to deliver beer. Originally horse-drawn.

Dreher Anton Dreher's name today only appears on an Italian brewing group jointly controlled by Heineken and Whitbread, but at the turn of the century his brewing empire was the largest in the world, with plants in Hungary, Czechoslovakia, Italy, and Austria, where he brewed the first bottom-fermented lager beer in 1841.

Drinking-up time The time allowed for consumption of the last drink of the session (afternoon or evening). Time allowed is 10 minutes in England and Wales, 15 in Scotland, 30 in Northern Ireland, and 15 in the Isle of Man.

Dripmat Another name for *Beermat*.

Drip Tray A metal or plastic tray fitted under beer taps to catch the overflow or slops.

Druid's Ale Silverthorne's strong cask ale (1072) from South Wales.

Drum Keg bitters from Davenports of Birmingham (1036.5) and Tetleys of Leeds (1034).

Drum Malting A malting system first developed in Britain in the 1950s, employing modification within enclosed tubular revolving drums.

Drybrough Scottish arm of Watneys, with a brewery in Edinburgh and 80 pubs plus large free trade. *Cask beers*: Pentland (1036), Eighty (1042). *Keg*: Light (1032), Scotch (1034), Heavy (1036), Burns Special (1036), Original (1042), Export (1043). *Bottled*: Light (1032), Export (1043), Private Reserve (1056). *Canned only*: Scottish Pride lager (1032).

Dry Hopping The addition of a small quantity of fresh hops to a cask as it is filled with beer. Dry hopping adds a further aroma and bitterness to the beer, subtly different from that provided by the hops boiled in the copper. The hops floating on the beer surface also give protection from airborne spoilage organisms.

DUB Dortmunder Union, the chief rival to DAB in Dortmund, best known for its Export and Siegel Pils. With Schultheiss of Berlin, it forms one of Germany's major brewing groups.

Dublin Pride Dempsey's bottled export ale (1040) for the United States.

Duchy Keg and bottled beer (1037) from St Austell, Cornwall. The keg was formerly called Extra.

Dunkel The German for dark, usually indicating a Münchner beer. *Hell* means pale.

Durham Ale Whitbread's cask bitter (1036) for the northeast from Castle Eden.

Duttons See *Chesters*.

Duty The tax, levied by the Customs and Excise department, on all of the beer that a brewer produces. The tax is proportional to the strength of the beer and amounts to about 40% of the wholesale price of beer.

Duvel The golden Belgian ale from the Moortgat brewery near Antwerp, described by expert Michael

Jackson as 'one of the world's greatest beers'. Duvel (devil) is a soft, bottle-conditioned ale – with a sudden punch from its 8.5 per cent alcohol.

[E]

E Worthington E – Bass's fading premium keg bitter (1041).

Eagle Cask bitter (1035) from Charles Wells of Bedford, who use an eagle as their trademark.

Eagle Brewery Non-brewing beer wholesale company in central Wales, which has recently taken over a small brewery. See *Powell*.

Earl's Cask best bitter (1048) from the Bridgewater Arms, Herts.

Early Doors A northern (especially Lancashire) expression for opening time, or early opening time!

Eastcote Ale Premium cask bitter (1041) from Banks & Taylor of Bedfordshire.

East Lancs Thwaites bottled pale ale (1036) from Blackburn.

Ebony See *Old Chester*.

Economiser An old style of beer engine, now only common in parts of the north. The beer overflowing the glass into the drip tray is re-cycled through the pump. It sounds unhealthy but laboratory tests have not proved it so. Also known as an *Autovac* (after a particular make).

Edelbrau Lees premium keg and bottled lager (1052) from Manchester.

EG Paine's strong draught and bottled ale (1047) from St Neots, named after the Eynesbury Giant, James Toller (1798–1818), who was 8ft 6ins tall.

1843 Arkell's premium lager (1042) from Swindon, named after the year when the Wiltshire brewery was founded.

Eighty Drybrough's 80/- ale (1042) from Edinburgh.

80/- Ale Scottish term for premium beers; see *Shilling System*. Usually 1040–1050 and light in colour. Sometimes referred to as 'Export'.

Einbeck The original home of German Bock beer, near Hanover, now has just one remaining brewery (owned by DUB-Schultheiss) producing the classic Einbecker Ur-Bock.

Einhorn Robinson's keg and bottled lager (1035) from Stockport. Einhorn is German for Unicorn, the brewery symbol.

Eisbock The strongest type of German Doppelbock, with an amazing alcohol content of over 12 per cent. It is made by partly freezing the beer (*Eis* means ice) and then, since water freezes before alcohol, removing ice to concentrate this very rich beer. The leading example is Kulminator.

EKU The Erste Kulmbacher Brewery of Bavaria (known as EKU) is famed for its Eisbock, Kulminator 28 Urtyp Hell, the strongest regularly-produced beer in the world.

Eldridge Pope Dorset brewers with 180 pubs, better known as Huntsman Ales, producing the strongest beer brewed in Britain, the bottle-conditioned Thomas Hardy Ale (1125). *Cask beers*: Dorchester Bitter (1032.5), Dorset Original IPA (1041), Royal Oak (1048). *Keg*: Mild (1030), Crystal Bitter (1034), Pope's 1880 (1041), Faust Pilsener (1035), Export Lager (1042). *Bottled*: Crystal Light (1030), Pope's 1880 (1041), Green Top (1042), Royal Oak (1048), Goldie (1085), Thomas Hardy (1125), Faust Pilsener (1035), Diät Pils (1035).

Electric Pump There are various means of electrically delivering the beer from a cask to the counter dispenser, all referred to as electric pumps. The two main types are free flow and metered positive displacement. Free flow pumps are of the impeller type: they are switched on by a pressure switch that senses a drop in beer line pressure when the tap is opened, and they continue to run until closing the tap causes a pressure pulse that resets the pressure switch. The displacement type pump has a calibrated half-pint container from which the beer is displaced whenever a push-button at the dispense point is pressed. Displacement metered pumps are measured and sealed by the Customs & Excise and consequently they may be used with unmarked glasses, unlike any other dispense method.

Elephant Carlsberg's well-known Danish export lager, named after the stone elephants at the Copenhagen brewery gate, which is imported into England as Carlsberg 68 (1062). The elephant is also the symbol of Whitbread Fremlins of Kent.

Elgood Fenland riverside brewery near the Wash in Wisbech, producing one distinctive real ale for half its 55 pubs. *Cask beer*: Bitter (1036). *Keg*: Fenman Bitter (1033), Mellow Mild (1032). *Bottled*: Brown Ale (1030), Pale Ale (1030), Russet Ale (1032), Fenman (1033).

Elizabethan Harvey's very powerful bottled barley wine (1090) from Sussex.

English Ale Whitbread's bottled beer (1042) specially brewed for diabetics as it is low in sugar.

Entire An early form of porter, properly called 'entire butts' to indicate that it was brewed to reproduce in one beer (and hence entirely in one cask or butt) the characteristics of three separate beers (pale ale, brown ale, and stock ale) sold in the early 18th century as 'three threads' or 'three thirds'. Each of the three beers was tapped in turn into the pot to give a mixture; this obviously required more time than if the beer was drawn from one cask, and hence in 1722 Ralph Harwood, a brewer in Shoreditch, hit on the idea of replacing 'three threads' with 'entire butts'. Name misleadingly used by Holt, Plant & Deakin for their premium cask bitter (1043).

ESB Extra Special Bitter (1055.75) in every sense from Fullers of London. Mitchells of Lancaster also brew a cask ESB (1044.8), but not to quite the same powerful strength.

Eskie Australian term for a portable thermos case used for keeping beer cool.

Essex Ale Ridley's bottled light ale (1030).

Everards Leicestershire company with 140 pubs and a small plant at Leicester brewing Old Original. Their old Burton brewery is now a working museum producing Tiger and Mild. Whitbread brew a disappointing Everards Bitter. *Cask beers*: Burton Mild (1033), Bitter (1035), Tiger (1041), Old Original (1050). *Keg*: As cask, apart from Original. *Bottled*: Red Crown (1034.3), Brown Ale (1033), Bitter (1033), Tiger (1041).

Ex-Beer Alcohol-free lager from the Swiss Feldschlosschen brewery, imported into Britain by North Country Breweries.

Excise See *Duty*.

Exhibition Newcastle's well-known cask and keg bitter (1042). Also Silverthorne's (1054) and Smiles (1051) strong cask beer, Border's light mild (1034), and Harvey's bottled strong brown ale (1042).

Exmoor Ale Golden Hill's award-winning cask bitter (1039) from Wiveliscombe, Somerset.

Export Term applied to premium beers that may or may not be exported. Name often interchangeable with IPA (India Pale Ale). In Scotland, Export may be keg brews or cask 80/- ales.

Export Gold Watney's bottled barley wine (1070).

Extra Powerful ale (1085) from Britain's most northerly brewery, Borve House, Isle of Lewis. Also Tennent's premium keg lager (1044), and former name for St Austell's Duchy keg bitter (1037) from Cornwall.

Extra Light Bass thin cask and keg bitter for the north (1031).

Extralite Low-gravity (1030) slimmers' bottled beer from Wadworth of Wiltshire.

Extra Special Bottled bitter (1038) from Simpkiss in the Black Country. See also *ESB*.

[F]

Failsworth Small Manchester brewery set up in 1982 next to the might of neighbouring Wilsons. Has one pub. *Cask beers*: Failsworth Original (1037), Strong (1044).

Falcon Allied's cheapie canned lager (1032). Produced only for Victoria Wine off-licences.

Falcon Ales Okell's beers from the Isle of Man.

Falmouth Devenish premium keg bitter (1038), named after Carne's Falmouth Brewery taken over in 1921.

Falstaff Tetley's cask and keg pale mild (1032), known as 'Best' or 'Scotch' depending on the area.

Family Ale An old name for light bitter beer, usually bottled.

Famous Taddy Porter Sam Smith's bottled porter (1050) for export from Tadcaster, Yorkshire.

Fargo Charles Wells bottled strong ale (1046) from Bedford, whose name once prompted legal action from the Wells Fargo company of America!

Farmer's Ale Oakhill cask bitter (1038) from near Bath. Also McMullen's bottled bitter (1036) from Hertford.

Farmer's Glory Distinctive stronger cask bitter (1046) from Wadworth of Devizes, introduced in 1984. Named after Wiltshire author A.G. Street's first book.

Farm Stout Greene King's bottled sweet stout (1035) from East Anglia.

Faro A diluted version of wild Lambic beer, sweetened with sugar. Rarely found in Belgium today.

Farsons Malta's sole brewery (full name Simonds Farsons Cisk) which, thanks to the island's former British connections, brews the only top-fermented ales in the Mediterranean: Blue Label, Hop Leaf, and Brewer's Choice. All are pasteurised.

Faust Eldridge Pope's keg and bottled Pilsener (1035) and Export (1042) lagers brewed in Dorchester under licence from the Faust (fist) brewery of Miltenberg,

Bavaria. Also bottled Diät Pils (1035).

Faxe Virtually the only Danish brewery to produce unpasteurised beer, notably Faxe Fad bottled lager (4.5 per cent alcohol). *Fad* means draught.

Federation The Northern Clubs Federation Brewery in Newcastle, popularly known as 'Fed', is one of only two specialist clubs breweries remaining in Britain. The other is Crown in South Wales. But, unlike Crown, Fed at its new Dunston plant produces only processed beers. *Tank*: Pale Mild (1033), Dark Mild (1033), Pale Ale (1033), Best Scotch (1036), Special Ale (1041), Special Bitter (1041), Medallion Lager (1036). *Keg*: As tank, plus Best Bitter (1036), Export (1047), Ace Lager (1032), LCL Pils (1036). *Bottled*: Special (1041), Sweet Stout (1043), Strong Brown (1047), Export (1047), LCL Pils (1036).

Felinfoel Britain's champion brewers in the past, though these famous Welsh beers from Llanelli are pressurised in the majority of their 75 pubs. Partly owned by neighbours Buckley. *Cask beers*: Mild (1032), Bitter (1034), Double Dragon (1041). *Keg*: Bitter (1034), Double Dragon (1041). *Bottled*: Nut Brown (1032), John Brown (1032), Bitter Ale (1034), Double Dragon (1041), Double Strong (1075). Chiefly for export: St. David's Porter (1036), Cream Stout (1040).

Fellows, Morton & Clayton Whitbread canalside home-brew pub (using malt extract) in Nottingham. *Cask beers*: Fellow's Bitter (1040), Clayton's Original (1048).

Fenman Elgood's keg and bottled bitter (1033) from Wisbech in the Fens.

Ferret & Firkin Bruce home-brew pub, London SW10. *Cask beers*: Stoat (1036), Ferret Ale (1045), Dogbolter (1060).

Fermentation The stage when yeast is added to the fermentation vessels to convert the wort into beer.

Festival Greenall Whitley's keg (1039) and bottled (1042) export. Also Burton Bridge strong draught ale (1055).

Festive King & Barnes strong pale ale (1050) from Sussex, on draught and in bottle.

Final Gravity See *Original Gravity*.

Fine To add finings to a cask or vessel.

Finings A glutinous syrup made from the swim bladders of a type of sturgeon fish found in the South China Sea (honestly!). Several pints of 'finings' are added to each cask of traditional beer to precipitate the yeast cells, leaving the beer 'bright'. Also known as *isinglass*.

Finish A term for the aesthetic appeal of a beer, similar to *polish*.

Firkin A 9-gallon cask. Also the common name of a chain of home-brew pubs in London, eg Goose & Firkin, Fox & Firkin.

Fisherman Adnams stronger bottled brown ale (1042) from Suffolk.

Five Star Home Brewery's premium keg bitter (1043) from Nottingham.

Five Towns Small Potteries brewery begun in 1983, now behind The Globe in Hanley, Staffs. *Cask beers*: Mild (1035), Bursley Bitter (1040), Bennet's Strong Ale (1057).

Five X Shepherd Neame's stronger cask winter warmer (1044) from Kent. See also *XXXXX*.

Fix Greece's best-known lager.

Flagon A quart bottle. The original takeaway container.

Flash Cooler A small refrigeration unit connected directly to the drink supply line near to the dispense tap, thus serving the drink at the required temperature without having to cool the bulk container. Flash coolers should never be used with cask-conditioned beers.

Fleece & Firkin Bruce home-brew pub in the old wool merchants' hall, Bristol, now owned by Halls. *Cask beers*: Bootlace (1038), Best Bristol (1045), Dogbolter (1060), Coal Porter (1048).

Flocculate In clarifying the beer the finings cause the yeast cells to clump together into fluffy lumps; this process is *flocculation*.

Floor Maltings The most traditional method of turning barley into malt. During germination, barley is evenly spread on a malting floor to a depth of around 8 inches and is turned over (often manually) to dispel excess heat and allow even respiration and germination.

Flounder & Firkin Bruce home-brew pub, London N7. *Cask beers*: Fish T'ale (1036), Whale Ale (1045), Dogbolter (1060).

Flowers Famous British brewing name resurrected by Whitbread for some of their southern beers, chiefly brewed at Cheltenham, and for their West Midlands trading company. The original brewery at Stratford-upon-Avon was closed in 1968. *Cask*: Flowers IPA (1036), Original (1044). *Keg*: Best Bitter (1035).

Fob Excessive and troublesome froth often seen when serving lager or keg beers. Fobbing can occur with Real Ale if there is an air leak in the connections to the cask.

Forest Keg lager (1038) from New Forest, Hants.

Forest Brown Whitbread's bottled brown ale (1032).

Forshaw See *Burtonwood*.

Fortyniner Ringwood premium cask bitter (1049) from Hampshire.

Fosters The ice-cold canned lager praised by every exiled Australian (from Victoria) is brewed by Carlton United of Melbourne, where it is one of many brands. It has an average Australian alcohol content of 4.8 per cent – and kangaroo hops, of course.

Fosters Draught The 'beer from down under' in Britain in fact comes from Watney's Mortlake plant in London. Odder still, Fosters lager is not traditionally produced on draught in Australia, where it is canned. Watney's mock Fosters (1035) is also weaker than the 1045 Aussie original.

Founder's Usher's premium cask ale (1045) from Wiltshire.

Four Keys Home-brew pub at Wadhurst, Sussex. *Cask beers*: 4K Bitter (1036), Stallion (1045).

Foursome Name used by Banks's of Wolverhampton for their large cans of mild or bitter.

4X Cask and keg milds from Border (1030) and Crown (1036). Also Burt's old ale (1040) bottled as 4X strong brown. See *XXXX*.

4XXXX Mansfield's premium cask bitter (1045).

Fowler's Wee Heavy Famous Scottish strong ale whose name has survived despite the original brewers, Fowlers of Prestonpans, being taken over in 1960 and later closed down. The bottled ale today is brewed by Belhaven of Dunbar for Tennent-Caledonian to the recipe for their own strong ale (1070).

Fox & Firkin Bruce home-brew pub, Lewisham, London. *Cask beers*: Vixen (1036), Bruce's Bitter (1045), Dogbolter (1060).

Fox & Hounds Home-brew pubs near Royston, Herts, and Stottesdon, Shropshire. The Royston one at Barley has a wooden sign stretching across the road showing a hunting scene. *Cask beers*: Nathaniel's Special (1034), Nog (1040), Hogshead (1043). The Shropshire one also sells Dasher's Draught (1040) in the free trade.

Fox & Newt Whitbread home-brew pub (using malt extract) in Leeds. *Cask beers*: Burley (1036), Old Willow (1046).

Framboise A Belgian Gueuze beer in which the second fermentation has been caused by adding raspberries.

Free Flow The usual way to serve a *keg* or *top pressure* beer. The pressurised keg is connected directly to a small on-off tap – beer flows freely as long as the tap is held open.

Free House A pub supposedly free of any brewery tie, and therefore able to offer a range of beers from different breweries. Term often abused nowadays.

Fremlins Whitbread's Kent brewery based in Faversham, with real ale in the vast majority of its 750 pubs. *Cask beer*: Fremlins Bitter (1037). *Keg*: AK (1032), Trophy (1035).

Friar's Ale Morrell's keg bitter (1036) from Oxford.

Friary Meux Ind Coope's southern Home Counties company with some 600 pubs, based in Godalming, Surrey. The original Friary brewery in Guildford closed in 1969, with the name revived in 1980. Beers are brewed at Romford and Burton. *Cask beer*: Bitter (1037). *Bottled*: Light Ale (1032), Treble Gold (1052).

Frisk Low-carbohydrate keg lager (1033) from Vaux of Sunderland.

Frog & Firkin Bruce home-brew pub, London W11. *Cask beers*: Tavistock (1036), Bullfrog (1045), Dogbolter (1060).

Frog & Frigate Southampton home-brew pub. *Cask beers*: Frog's Original (1040), Croaker (1050).

Frog & Parrot Whitbread home-brew pub (using malt extract) in Sheffield. *Cask beers*: Old Croak (1035), Reckless Bitter (1046), Roger's Special (1065).

Froth The bubbles on the top of a glass, more often known as the head. The *Ancient Order of Frothblowers* were an informal organisation of pub-goers, active in the 1930s, mixing social activities with the collection of large sums for children's charities.

Fruh (Colner Hofbrau) Famous home-brew house opposite Cologne Cathedral, serving a fine example of the city's own beer, Kolsch, now brewed off the premises.

Fruit Machine Known in the trade as AWP (amusements with prizes), electronic gambling machines giving small prizes (in pubs) with disastrously low odds on winning; now much more sophisticated and noisy than the original 'one-armed bandit'.

FSB Firkin Special Brew (1058) from the Bosham Brewery, West Sussex.

Fullers One of London's two famous independent family brewers, brewing a fine range of beers by the Thames at Chiswick for their 127 pubs, including the revered ESB. *Cask beers*: Chiswick Bitter (1035.5), London Pride (1041.5), ESB (1055.75). *Keg*: Mild (1035.5), Bitter (1035.5), London Pride (1041.5). *Bottled*: Brown Ale (1032), Pale Ale (1032), London Pride (1045), Golden Pride (1090).

Fun Pub A phenomenon of the 1980s, where the music is louder, the lights brighter, and the customers more youthful than at the pub down the road. An odd concept, as *all* pubs should be fun.

Fussell's Bass's cask bitter (1038) for the southwest, brewed in Cardiff. Named after the Somerset brewery taken over in 1962.

[G]

Gales Traditional Hampshire brewery in Horndean with a rare range of real ales for its 97 pubs, especially the powerful HSB and the even more potent Prize Old Ale, Britain's only naturally-conditioned beer in a corked bottle. *Cask beers*: XXXL (1030), XXXD (1032), BBB (1037), XXXXX (1044), HSB (1051). *Keg*: Treble Seven (1034), Southdown Bitter (1040). *Bottled*: Nut Brown (1032), Pale Ale (1031), Nourishing Stout (1034), Champion Ale (1040), Tudor Ale (1051), Prize Old Ale (1095).

Gallon The basis of the imperial system of liquid measure, a gallon is the volume of 10 lbs of distilled water. A gallon is eight pints, the metric equivalent is 4.54 litres. The US gallon is four-fifths of the British one. 'Play for the gallon' is a common expression in pub games where each losing team member has to buy a drink for his opponent.

Gate (1) Whitbread home-brew pub (using malt extract) in Southampton. *Cask beers*: Three Bar (1035), Five Bar (1050). **(2)** Home-brew pub, The Lee, Bucks. *Cask beer*: Carr's Best Bitter (1041).

GB Lees mild (1032) from Manchester. The initials stand for Greengate Brewery.

Genesee The main producers of American Cream Ale (4.75 per cent alcohol), from Rochester, New York. The company also brews a stronger ale called Twelve Horse.

George's Haverfordwest family company revived by Ansells in 1981 to handle their West Wales beer wholesale business. Has its own keg bitter, George's Best (1037), brewed in Burton.

George's Home-Brewed Courage bottled pale ale for the southwest (1042), named after the Bristol brewery Courage took over in 1961.

Gibberellic Acid A sugar-based natural acid added to the steeping water in order to encourage embryo development in the malting process. Also the main component of many lawn weedkillers!

Gibbs Mew Unusual Wiltshire brewery in Salisbury which not only runs many of its 85 pubs like free houses, but also owns Seymour soft drinks in Sherborne. *Cask beers*: Wiltshire Bitter (1036), Premium (1039), Salisbury Best (1042), Bishop's Tipple (1066). *Keg*: SPA (1031), Super Mild (1031), Wiltshire Special (1036), Anchor or Chairman's Choice (1039). *Bottled*: Pale Ale (1031), Moonraker Brown (1032), Sarum Special (1048), Bishop's Tipple (1066).

Gill (1) A quarter of a pint. Most frequently used to indicate spirit measures. The 'optics' in England are generally a sixth of a gill, and in Scotland a fifth. **(2)** Slang term for any drink, as in 'Let's go for a gill'. **(3)** Term used – wrongly – for a half pint of beer in Lancashire and Yorkshire.

Gin Palace A style of pub whose origins coincide with the popularity of gin in the 19th century, consequent upon a reduction in duty on spirits. Flamboyant and often gaudy in style, rich in ornament and decoration; a contrast with the (then) squalid public house. Try the magnificent Barton's Arms, Birmingham; or the Philharmonic, Liverpool.

Glass A half pint of beer (used especially in Ireland).

Glenny Small Oxfordshire brewery set up in 1983 in part of Clinch's old brewery in Witney. *Cask beers*: Witney Bitter (1037), Wychwood Best (1044).

Globe Home-brew pub (using malt extract) in Fishguard, Wales. *Cask beer*: Black Fox (1038).

Goacher Small Kent brewery set up in 1983 to revive Maidstone's once-proud brewing tradition. *Cask beers*: Maidstone Light (1036), Maidstone Ale (1040), Goacher's 1066 (1066).

Godson Chudley Two of the pioneers of the new brewery movement in London merged in 1984, brewing on one site at Bow but still producing two ranges of real ales: Godson's Black Horse (1048), Stock Ale (1085), Wilmot's Hop Cone (1042), and Chudley's Local Line (1038), Lord's Strong (1048), Draught Excluder (1070). *Bottled*: Stock Ale (1085).

Gold Buckley's stronger keg bitter (1043) from South Wales, besides premium lagers from Tuborg (1045), Grunhalle (1045), and Amstel of Holland.

Gold Eagle Charles Wells keg bitter (1034) from Bedford.

Golden Archers premium cask ale (1050) from Swindon. Also Holden's keg and bottled pale ale (1039) from the Black Country.

Golden Ale Cook's bottled light ale (1030) brewed by Ridleys of Essex.

Golden Best Timothy Taylor's fine light mild (1033) from Keighley, Yorkshire, sometimes known as Bitter Ale.

Golden Hill Small Somerset brewery at Wiveliscombe with the unique distinction of winning an award at CAMRA's Great British Beer Festival only months after starting in 1980. *Cask beer*: Exmoor Ale (1039).

Golden IPA Burt's Ventnor Pale Ale (1040) in bottle from the Isle of Wight.

Golden Pride Fuller's powerful bottled pale ale (1090), which makes ESB seem like a mild drink.

Golden Promise A strain of barley regarded as the best quality for ale malt, grown in Scotland.

Goldie Bottled barley wine (1085) from Eldridge Pope of Dorset – named after the golden eagle which escaped from London Zoo!

Golding Ale King & Barnes pale barley wine (1075) from Sussex, named after the famous Golding hop.

Gold Label Whitbread's powerful pale barley wine (1098), now again being brewed in its home town of Sheffield. A classic example of the style, though in danger of destroying all the other brands. Also the name of Whitbread's keg Yorkshire lager (1036).

Gold Star Bottled light ale (1034) from Shipstone of Nottingham.

Goods The contents of the mash tun – malt plus any

other grains or adjuncts.

Goose & Firkin Bruce's first home-brew pub, set up in Southwark, London, in 1979. The only one to use malt extract. *Cask beers*: Goose Ale (1036), Borough (1045), Dogbolter (1060).

Goose Eye Colourful small brewery in a mill near Keighley, Yorkshire, since 1978, with one pub, the Turkey Inn, opposite. *Cask beers*: Bitter (1038), Special or Wharfdale Ale (1045), Pommie's Revenge (1060).

Gordons Besides being a well-known gin, Gordons is a very strong bottled ale (9.5 per cent alcohol) brewed by Scottish & Newcastle – for sale to the Belgians.

Goudenband Speciaal Provisie Bottle-conditioned ale from Liefmans of Belgium, described by expert Michael Jackson as 'the world's finest brown ale' (6.5 per cent alcohol). There are also a commoner Oudenaarde Speciaal (5.25) and a cherry Kriek (7.5), both based on Provisie.

Government Stamped Any glass used in a pub for draught beer or cider has to have been tested by the Customs and Excise and must bear the tester's mark – the crown and a number.

Granary Cask bitter (1038) from Reepham Brewery, Norfolk.

Grand Cru The premium version of the unique Belgian white beer, Hoegaards Wit, with an alcohol content of 7.5 per cent.

Grandma A mixed pint, either old and mild or else (Midlands) sweet stout and old. See *Mother-in-Law*.

Grand Metropolitan Hotel and leisure giant which owns one of Britain's 'Big Six' national brewers, Watney Mann Truman. Also owns Express Dairies (Ski/ Eden Vale), International Distillers & Vintners (J&B Scotch/Gilbey's Gin/Croft Sherry/Peter Dominic off-licences), Inter-Continental and Forum Hotels, Mecca, Warner's holidays, plus US food, drinks, and tobacco interests.

Gravity (1) A method of serving beer direct from a cask behind the bar. **(2)** A measure of the density of beer. See *Original Gravity*.

Gray Chelmsford company which has ceased brewing

and now supplies its 50 Essex pubs with Greene King draught beers.

Great British Beer Festival An annual celebration of traditional British beers run by unpaid CAMRA volunteers, who man the biggest bar in the world for a week, serving 250 different real ales. National Festivals have been held in London, Birmingham, Leeds, and Brighton.

Great Northern Wilson's keg and canned bitter (1036) from Manchester.

Great Western Crown Brewery's premium keg bitter (1041) from South Wales. Also the only successful commercial beer festival in Britain, held in Bristol every year.

Greenall Whitley Britain's largest regional brewery, based in Warrington, with over 1,000 pubs in the northwest, besides owning Shipstone of Nottingham and Wem of Shropshire. Increasingly involved in processed beer and the export market. *Cask beers*: Mild (1033.7), Local Bitter (1038), Original Bitter (1040). *Keg*: Mild and Bitter (also in tank), plus Scotch (1032), Special (1037), Festival (1039), Haagen Lager (1032), Grunhalle (1035), Grunhalle Export (1045). *Bottled*: Bulls Eye Brown (1035), Champion Pale Ale (1038), Red Rose Stout (1040), Festival Export (1042), Old Chester (1067), Old Glory (1074), Greenall's Lager (1032), Grunhalle (1038), DB Pils (1038), Grunhalle Export (1045). The stronger bottled beers are also exported under a wide variety of names.

Green Beer Young beer at the end of primary fermentation or beer that has not had long enough to mature in the cask; such beer has a coarse, unpleasant flavour. Unfortunately, economic pressures are tempting brewers and licensees to sell ever younger beer.

Green Death See *Rainier*.

Greene King East Anglian giants with 780 pubs and three breweries in Bury St Edmunds, Suffolk; Biggleswade, Beds; and Furneux Pelham, Herts (Rayments). Famous for their potent Abbot Ale and remarkable family which includes the novelist Graham Greene and the former director general of the BBC, Sir Hugh Greene. *Cask beers*: XX Dark Mild (1031), KK Light Mild (1031), IPA (1035), Abbot (1048), Christmas Ale (1052). *Keg*: King Keg (1038), Yeoman (1038), Abbot (1048). *Bottled*: Pale Ale (1031), Harvest Brown (1031), Burton Ale (1031), Farm Stout (1035), Crown (1039), Abbot (1048), Strong Suffolk (1056), St Edmund (1060). See also *Rayment*.

Green Label Wadworth's bottled 6X (1040) from Wiltshire (canned as Best Bitter). Also Webster's keg and tank light mild, popularly known as 'Best' (1034), from Halifax. A stronger version (1038) is sold in bottle and can.

Green Malt Term applied to barley after modification and prior to kilning.

Greenmantle Broughton's cask and bottled ale (1038) from Scotland.

Green Top Eldridge Pope's bottled export pale ale (1042) from Dorset.

Greyhound Clifton Inns home-brew pub, Streatham, London SW16. *Cask beers*: Greyhound Special (1037), Streatham Strong (1047).

Grimbergen Abbaye-style beer from the Maes brewery of Belgium – owned by Watneys.

Grist Malted barley, the main ingredient of the mash, has to be milled ('cracked') into a coarse powder to allow the fermentable materials to be extracted. The cracked malt is the *grist*.

Grist Case A large hopper that contains the ground malt (grist). In a traditional tower brewery the grist case is on the upper floor above the mash tun into which the grist is dropped.

Grog Australian term for alcoholic beverage.

Grog Blossom Slang term for a heavy drinker's red nose.

Grolsch Dutch brewery from Groenlo, internationally renowned for its distinctive pot-stoppered, embossed bottle. The Pilsener inside is equally traditional, being unpasteurised and conditioned for two months.

Grunhalle Lager 'brewed the Bavarian way', devised by Edward Greenall (Grunhalle means green hall), Chairman of Randalls Vautier of Jersey. Randalls first brewed the beer and then Grunhalle International of Jersey licensed the much larger (and related) Greenall Whitley of Warrington to produce *keg* Grunhalle (1035), Export Gold (1045) and *bottled* Grunhalle (1038), DB Pils (1038), and Export Gold (1045). Also brewed by Devenish.

Guernsey Brewery Delightfully set in the harbour of St Peter Port, this Channel Island firm produces stronger than average 'Pony Ales' for its 30 pubs, owing to excise duty being levied on quantity not strength. *Cask beers*: LBA Mild (1037.7), Draught Bitter (1045). *Keg*: Best Bitter (1045), Stein (1048). *Bottled*: Pony Ale (1037.7), Brown Ale (1038), Milk Stout (1042), IPA (1045), Stein (1048).

Gueuze A blend of wild Lambic beers from Belgium which ferments again to form a stronger, fruitier brew (5.5 per cent alcohol), sometimes conditioned for years. Good examples include Lindemans and Timmermans. The most commercial is Belle Vue.

Guinea Gold Hardys & Hansons bottled light ale (1032) from Nottingham.

Guinness World-famous Irish stout brewers, who operate 14 breweries around the world in Eire, London, Africa, Malaysia, and Jamaica, with brewing contracts in another 24 countries. Also control Irish Ale Breweries and Harp. *Keg*: Draught Guinness (1037.4). *Bottled*: Extra Stout (1042). The draught is keg (though not pasteurised in Eire), while the stronger bottled, in returnable bottles, is naturally conditioned. A heavier Foreign Extra Stout (8 per cent alcohol), once marketed in Britain as Triple X, is brewed abroad and in Dublin for export.

Gush The same as *Fob*.

Gwent Ales See *Silverthorne*.

Gyle The batch of beer from one brewing. Casks are usually identified with a 'gyle number' or date code.

Gypsum Hydrated calcium sulphate – the chief mineral constituent of Burton-upon-Trent well water, ideal for making bitter beers. See *Burtonise*.

[H]

Haagen Greenall Whitley's weak keg lager (1032) from Warrington.

Hacker-Pschorr One of the leading German breweries in Munich, along with Spaten, Paulaner, HB, Augustiner, and Lowenbrau.

Half Don't ask for this in Scotland or Ireland, as you will not get a half-pint of beer, but instead a measure of whisky/whiskey.

Half-and-half An equal mixture of two beers in a pint, usually mild and bitter.

Hall & Woodhouse Dorset family brewery since 1777, known for its 'Badger Beers'. Besides running 155 pubs, the Blandford Forum company specialises in canned beer and soft drinks under the Panda name. *Cask beers*: Hector's Bitter (1034), Badger Best (1041), Tanglefoot (1048). *Keg*: Malthouse (1033), Badger Export (1037), Badger Best (1041), Brock Lager (1033). *Bottled*: John Brown (1031), Stingo (1066). *Canned*: Skona Lager (1032).

Hall Cross See *Stocks*.

Hallerbrau Filtered but unpasteurised summer lager (1042) from Phillips, Bucks.

Hallertau The most famous German hops from Bavaria.

Hall's Former Oxford brewery which ceased brewing in 1952. The name was revived in 1980 to cover Allied's 350 West Country pubs. Hall's cask Harvest Bitter (1037) and keg Barleycorn (1033) are brewed at Burton; bottled light and brown ales (1032) are brewed by

Wadworth. In 1984/5 Hall's also set up two small breweries in its Avon and Devon depots producing cask beer: Hall's Bristol Brewery – Jacob's Best (1038), Bristol Pride (1045); Hall's Plympton Brewery – Plympton Best (1039), Plympton Pride (1039).

Hammerhead Clark's strong ale (1050) from Wakefield, Yorks.

Hancock Cardiff brewery taken over by Bass in 1968 and now operating as Welsh Brewers. Still retains some 'Hancock' draught beers – Pale Ale (1033) and HB (1037).

Handle A glass mug with a handle.

Handpump The more usual name for the *beer engine*, since it is the part customers see in the bar; also sometimes known as a *handpull*. The sign of Real Ale.

Hannen Most widely available brand of Alt, the German dark ale, produced at three breweries around Düsseldorf, with an alcohol content of 4.5 per cent.

Hansa Part of the DAB group in Dortmund, this German brewery licenses Camerons of Hartlepool to brew its lager to a weaker recipe (1036).

Hanson's The smaller part of Wolverhampton and Dudley Breweries, the Black Country giant, which brews similar cask beers at Dudley to Banks's in Wolverhampton. Not to be confused with Hardys & Hansons of Nottingham. *Cask beers*: Mild (1036), Bitter (1038). See *Banks's*.

Happy Day Scottish term for a pint, made up with ⅔ pt of Light or 60/- ale together with a 'Wee Heavy', a nip-sized bottle of strong ale.

Hardington Somerset brewery which started in Hardington Mandeville in 1979 and moved to the Brewers Arms, South Petherton, in 1984. Supplies its own pub and local free trade. *Cask beers*: Best Bitter (1036.5), Somerset Special (1043). *Keg*: Landsdorf Lager (1034).

Hardy's Ale See *Thomas Hardy's Ale*.

Hardys & Hansons Nottingham family brewery, the result of a merger in 1930 between two neighbouring firms in Kimberley, with 200 pubs, many using top pressure. *Cask beers*: Best Mild (1035.4), Best Bitter (1038.6). *Keg*: As cask. *Bottled*: Guinea Gold (1032),

Special Brown (1036), Starbright IPA (1039), Blackamoor Stout (1044).

Harp One of the earliest British-brewed lagers, originally set up by a consortium of brewers. Now Harp is
owned by Guinness (75%) and Greene King (25%) and
brewed at Park Royal (London) and Dundalk (Eire)
and, under licence, by Scottish & Newcastle and
Courage. *Keg*: Harp (1032), Harp Special (1041), Harp
Export (1047.5), Kronenbourg 1664 (1046). *Bottled*:
Harp (1032), Satzenbrau (1047).

Hartley Cumbrian brewery at Ulverston famous for its
'Beers from the Wood', taken over by Robinsons of
Stockport in 1982. Still brewing real ale for its 54 pubs.
Cask beers: Mild (1031), Bitter (1031), XB (1040).

Hartsman McMullen's lager (1035) from Hertford.

Harty Small Irish brewery at Blessington, southwest of
Dublin. Began in 1983 brewing real ale but now produces only keg Harty's lager (1039).

Harvest Hall's cask bitter (1037) for the West
Country, brewed at Burton. Also Greene King bottled
brown ale (1031).

Harvey Sussex family brewery with 30
pubs and a fine Victorian Gothic
brewery by the river in the ancient
town of Lewes. Has also brewed for
Beards of Lewes since the 1950s. *Cask
beers*: XX Mild (1030), Pale Ale (1033),
Best Bitter (1040), XXXX Old Ale
(1043). *Keg*: Sussex Keg (1038). *Bottled*: Nut Brown
(1030), Sussex Stout (1030), IPA (1033), Blue Label
(1038), Exhibition Brown (1042), Elizabethan (1090),
Christmas Ale (1090).

Haze A lack of clarity in beer; a milkiness in which no
actual particles can be seen. See *Chill*.

HB Hancock's Bitter (1037) from Welsh Brewers,
Cardiff.

HB (Hofbrauhaus) The State-owned former royal
brewery of Bavaria, which, besides its famous Munich
beer hall, developed German Bock beer. Its Maibock is
a classic of its style. HB also popularised Weizenbier
(wheat beer) in South Germany, producing an excel-

lent Edel-Weizen today.

HE Ridley's premium cask bitter (1045), introduced in 1983. The initials stand for Hartford End, the Essex hamlet which hides this Victorian brewery.

Head The froth on the top of a glass of beer. Drinkers in some areas consider the nature of the head to be almost as important as the quality of the beer itself. The West Yorkshire area is the noted example; a pint served there without a *tight head* would be rejected. A tight head is obtained by forcing the beer through very small orifices in the sparkler on the pump, making a stiff creamy foam of almost invisibly small bubbles. The beer is drunk 'through' the head, which should persist until all of the beer has been drunk. In most of the north of England and Scotland beer is served with a large head, whilst most of the southern area prefers the *loose head* – a light froth of large irregular bubbles which rapidly collapse.

Headbanger Aptly-named strong cask ale (1065) from Archers of Swindon.

Heavitree Devon company which ceased brewing in 1970, and now supplies its 120 pubs around Exeter with beers from Whitbread, Bass, and Eldridge Pope.

Heavy Scottish term for medium gravity beer, usually 1034–39. Otherwise known as 70/- ale. Confusingly, 'heavy' is usually light in colour, whereas 'light' is dark. Do not mix with a 'Wee Heavy', a nip of Scottish barley wine.

Hector's Cask bitter (1034) from Hall & Woodhouse of Dorset, named after John Hector's brewery taken over in 1883.

Heel Taps Any dregs left in a nominally empty glass. Presumably derived from the same expression used for the small segment of leather used to mend a shoe heel.

Heineken This Dutch lager really does refresh the parts other beers cannot reach . . . as it is brewed in 20 countries. It is probably the best-known brand in the world, and is also the leading beer imported by the USA. The 'Heineken' brewed under licence in Britain by Whitbread is a pale imitation (1033), considerably weaker than the Amsterdam original. Bottled Export

(1048) is imported.

Heldenbrau Whitbread's weak keg and bottled lager (1032) for the northwest.

Hell The German for pale (*dunkel* is dark), which can lead to some odd beer names like Convikt Hell. Often used to order a pale Munchner.

Hemeling Bass's light keg and bottled lager (1030.7).

Henchard Premium cask bitter (1045) from Bourne Valley Brewery, Hampshire.

Henley Brewery name often shown outside Brakspear's Thames Valley pubs. See *Brakspear*.

Henninger Internationally-known Frankfurt brewery, whose bottled Henninger Pils (1044) is now imported into Britain by Courage.

Henry Boon Clark's Wakefield Ale (1038.5), named after the Yorkshire brewery's founder, Henry Boon Clark, who also gives his name to the brewery tap.

Herald Northern Ireland's second small free trade brewery, set up in Coleraine in 1983, though the cask beer, Herald Ale (1036), is usually sold under blanket pressure.

Hercules American export name for Felinfoel's bottled Double Strong (1075) from South Wales.

Herefordshire Ales New brewery set up in 1985 in Hereford. *Cask beers*: Olde Mild Ale (1035), Hereford Bitter (1038).

Herforder North German brewers have developed the brewing of Pilsener to produce a very dry lager like Herforder Pils (4.9 per cent alcohol).

Heriot Brewery Tennent's cask 80/- ale, named after their Edinburgh brewery.

Heritage Cask bitter (1036) from Phillips, Bucks. Also Whitbread home-brew pub, Cardiff, producing malt extract Heritage Ale (1038).

Hermitage Small brewery attached to the Sussex Brewery pub, Hermitage, West Sussex, since 1981, supplying the pub and local free trade. *Cask beers*: Mild (1034), Bitter (1040), Triple X (1044), Best Bitter (1048), Lumley Old Ale (1050).

Hicks Special Strong cask beer (1050) named after the 1851 founder of the St Austell Brewery in Cornwall, Walter Hicks.

Highgate Unique mild-only brewery within the Bass, Mitchells & Butlers empire at Walsall. *Cask beers*: Highgate Mild (1036), Best (1036), Old (1055).

High Gravity Brewing A modern development aimed at economising on brewery plant and material handling costs. Very strong beer is brewed and this is then watered down to the desired gravity when it is put into casks. Many brewers have experimented with this idea but have often been disappointed with the flavour of the resulting beers. Not at present in widespread use.

High Life Ind Coope's cheap bottled lager (1032) from Romford.

Higsons As much a part of Liverpool as the Beatles and football, Higson is Scouse city's only independent brewery, with 160 pubs. Built a new brewhouse in the early 1980s. *Cask beers*: Mild (1032), Bitter (1038). *Keg*: As cask, plus Higson's Lager (1036). *Bottled*: Double Top (1033), Pale Ale (1036), Stingo (1078). *Canned*: Prost Lager (1031).

Hilden Pioneer of real ale in Northern Ireland, when the brewery was set up in Lisburn, near Belfast, in 1981. *Cask beers*: Hilden Ale (1040), Winter Reserve (1044). *Keg*: Hildenbrau lager (1042). *Bottle*: Hilden Ale (1040) – naturally conditioned in bottle.

Hilton Name of breweries in two Kent home-brew pubs: Pier Hotel, Gravesend and Southeastern, Strood. *Cask beers*: Pirate Porter (1036), Clipper (1040), Grave-digger (1050), Buccaneer (1065), Lifebuoy (1075).

HOB Hoskins & Oldfield cask bitter (1041), Leicester.

Hock Former name for Fuller's Mild from London.

Hoegaards Wit The only existing Belgian white beer, from the De Kluis brewery near Louvain. Brewed from wheat and oats, and garnished with coriander and curaçao, this distinctive brew is stronger than Berliner Weisse. An ungarnished version, Peeterman, and a premium, Grand Cru, are also produced.

Hof Carlsberg's premium lager brewed in Britain (1042).

Hofmeister Courage's keg lager (1036), with the teddy bear image and no German pedigree despite the name. Canned Hofmeister is weaker at 1032.

Hogshead A 54-gallon cask, now fairly uncommon although some northern brewers still use them. A full wooden hogshead weighs more than a third of a ton!

Holden One of the small family breweries of the Black Country at Woodsetton, near Dudley, brewing a fine range of real ales for their 16 pubs. *Cask beers*: Mild (1036), Black Country Bitter (1039), Special (1052), Old Ale (1080). *Keg*: Mild (1036), Golden (1039). *Bottled*: Brown Ale (1036), Golden Pale (1039), Master Ale (1080).

Holsten Known in Britain for its bottled Diät Pils (1045), a strong dry lager from Hamburg, this company is the largest in North Germany, with breweries in several cities. Its most notable product is Moravia Pils. Keg Holsten Export lager (1045) in Britain is brewed by Watneys.

Holt Manchester family brewers of one of Britain's most distinctive bitters. Real ale in all 90 pubs, often delivered in hogsheads – such is the demand. *Cask beers*: Mild (1033), Bitter (1039). *Keg*: Holtenbrau (1033), Regal Lager (1039). *Bottled*: Pale Ale (1036), Brown Stout (1040), Sixex (1064).

Holtenbrau Holt's light lager (1033) from Manchester.

Holt, Plant & Deakin Ansells small Black Country company set up in 1984 to run 15 highly traditional pubs, with two cask beers – Holts Mild (1036.5) and Bitter (1036.5) – brewed by Tetley-Walker in Warrington, and a premium bitter, Entire (1043), brewed in their own small brewery at Oldbury.

Home Nottingham's largest brewery, with real ale in most of the 460 pubs stretching from Peterborough throughout the East Midlands to South Yorkshire. *Cask* *beers*: Mild (1036), Bitter (1038). *Keg*: Mild (1036), Five Star (1043). *Bottled*: Luncheon Ale (1034), Home Brewed (1036), Stout (1037), Robin Hood (1045), Centenary (1060), Little John (1070).

Home Brewed Home Brewery of Nottingham's bottled brown ale (1036).

Home-Brew House A pub which brews its own ale. Up to the beginning of this century, these were commonplace, but by the early 1970s only four survived. However, the real ale boom has encouraged licensees and major breweries alike to install small home-brew plants in pubs, and such brews as Nog, Dogbolter, and Paradise now enrich drinkers' choice and pleasure.

Hook Ale Bottled mild (1032) from Hook Norton (see below).

Hook Norton Probably the best remaining example in Britain of a Victorian tower brewery. This Oxfordshire family company near Banbury still brews a range of good-value real ales for its 34 pubs and and extensive free trade. *Cask beers*:  Mild (1032), Best Bitter (1036), Old Hookey (1049). *Bottled*: Hook Ale (1032), Jack Pot (1036), Jubilee (1049).

Hop The hop plant is a perennial from the Cannabaceae family – a group that includes both the nettle and cannabis. The brewers' hop, *Humulus lupulus*, grows as a climbing vine (always clockwise!) trained along frameworks of poles and wire. The harvested plant is the flower head. The flowers carry minute granules of yellow resin, lupulin, which contain the aromatic compounds that give the hop its bittering and preserving power. The main bitter agent is alpha acid. Before use by the brewer, hops are dried and packed into large sacks, called pockets. Such hops are bulky and perishable, so frequently now hops are ground, pressed into small pellets, and hermetically sealed. A more controversial practice is the extraction of the active chemicals as an oil. Many people consider that the flavour imparted by hop oil is inferior to that from full or pelletised hops. Some popular hop types are: Fuggles and Goldings, old-fashioned English varieties; Wye Challenger and Northdown, new high-Alpha strains bred at Wye agricultural college; and Target, a powerful hop which is also resistant to the fungus disease, Wilt, which is currently attacking English hop fields.

Hop Back After the wort has been boiled with the hops in the copper, the liquor is transferred to the fermenting vessels. In the transfer it passes through the hop back which filters out the spent hops together with any coagulated protein. The traditional hop back is a flat vessel with a perforated false floor, but modern ones often separate the residues centrifugally ('whirlpools').

Hop Bine The hop plant.

Hop Cone The hop flower head.

Hopfenperle North Country Breweries of Hull brew this lager under licence from the Swiss giant Feldschlosschen group.

Hop Garden The Kentish name for a hop field.

Hop Kiln The hop drying house, more often known as an oast house.

Hop Leaf Farsons pale ale (1040) from Malta. The name betrays the island brewery's earlier links with Simond's Hop Leaf brewery of Reading. Courage, which took over Simonds, still has a share stake in Farsons.

Hop Oil A chemical extract of the active components of the hop flower.

Hop Pellet Pulverised and pressed hop flowers.

Hop Pillow A pillow stuffed with fresh hops, sleep-inducing since some of the aromatic oils in the hop flowers have narcotic effects.

Hop Pocket A very large sack containing fresh hops – 1½ cwt.

Hop Yard The Southwest Midlands name for a hop field.

Horsing See *Stillage*.

Hoskins Old family brewery in Leicester which changed hands in

1983 and is now being expanded. Currently has three pubs, including the Thomas Hoskins at the brewery. *Cask beers*: Bitter (1039), Old (1039), Penn's Ale (1045), Old Nigel (1060). *Bottled*: IPA (1039).

Hoskins & Oldfield Small Leicester brewery set up in 1984 by a member of the Hoskins family who used to run the brewery above. *Cask beer*: HOB Bitter (1041).

Host Modern-day term used by the trade press to refer to licensees and their spouses.

Hostelry Originally a public house offering accommodation; synonymous with an inn. Now used somewhat pretentiously for any pub.

Hotel An establishment, licensed or unlicensed, offering accommodation and full meal service for travellers.

Hot Liquor The hot water that is poured onto the grain in the mash tun; see *Liquor*.

House of Horrors Early 1980s pub phenomenon popularised by Whitbread. Take a stuffed gorilla, a wickerwork frog, half a tailor's dummy, a tractor wheel, and pray that the customers put up with it for more than two weeks.

Hoxton Heavy Cask premium bitter (1048) from Pitfield Brewery, London N1.

HSB Horndean Special Bitter (1051) from Hampshire was introduced in 1959 by Gales head brewer, Ted Argyle, based on the strong Bass he had sampled in his home town of Burton-upon-Trent. Today Gales means HSB, one of the south's distinctive cask beers.

Hugget Scottish term for a *Hogshead*.

Hull Brewery See *North Country*.

Huntsman Ales The popular name for Eldridge Pope's beers and pubs in Dorset. The huntsman figure is also used by Tetleys in the north; both breweries adopted the design for use in their areas in the 1920s, but in 1935 E.P. redrew the jovial character with the monocle to avoid confusion.

Hurlimann Switzerland's best-known brewery, based in Zürich, which brews the world's strongest beer, Samichlaus (Santa Claus), containing a mighty 14 per cent alcohol. The more modest Hurlimann Sternbrau is brewed under licence in England by Shepherd Neame.

Hydes The smallest of Manchester's long-established independent family breweries, serving real 'Anvil' ales in all 50 tied houses, largely in the south of the city. *Cask beers*: Mild (1032), Best Mild (1034), Bitter (1036.6), Anvil Strong (1080). *Keg*: Bitter (1036.6), Amboss Lager (1036).

[I]

Ice Cold Australian term for a glass of lager.

Imperial Tetley's premium keg bitter (1042) for the northeast.

Imperial Old Ale Banks's dark barley wine (1096) from Wolverhampton. One of the strongest beers in Britain, only available in nip-size bottles.

Imperial Pale Maclay's bottled pale ale (1030) from Alloa, Scotland.

Imperial Russian Stout See *Russian Stout*.

Ind Coope One of the earliest national brewers, with breweries in Romford and Burton, which in 1961 merged with Ansells and Tetley Walker to form Allied Breweries. In the southeast the once ubiquitous name is now masked by a host of revived companies like Benskins, Friary Meux, Romford Brewery, and Taylor Walker. The east is handled by Ind Coope Allsopp and Burton Brewery. *Cask beers*: Bitter (1037), Burton Ale (1047.5). *Keg*: Drum Mild (1032), Pale (1033), Diamond Bitter (1033), Special (1037), Double Diamond (1037), Arctic Lite (1032), Skol (1037), Skol Special (1046), Allsopps Export (1046). *Bottled*: Light (1032), Brown (1033), Trent Bitter (1032), Trent Mild (1033), Double Diamond (1043), Arctic Lite (1032), Skol (1035), Skol Special (1046), Allsopps Export (1046). *Export only*: Pale Ale (1053), John Bull (1053). *Canned only*: Falcon (1032). All brewed at Burton, which also brews for ABC, Ansells, Georges, and Halls. See also *Romford* and *Wrexham*.

India Pale Ale Originally applied to strong pale ales of high keeping qualities and remarkable yeast stability, brewed to mature and come into condition (in cask) on the long sea voyage to India. Tradition has it that the fame of Bass as a brewer rests on the accidental shipwreck of a consignment of Bass's Pale Ale bound from Liverpool to India; the casks were retrieved and drunk eagerly, creating immediate home demand for more. The term is now debased by being applied to draught bitters of relatively ordinary qualities, often designated simply by the initials IPA.

Infusion The British method of mashing, i.e. extracting the fermentable material from the grist simply by leaving it to soak in the hot liquor for several hours. See also *Decoction*.

Inn Traditionally a licensed hostelry catering for travellers or wayfarers.

Inn Sign A signboard outside a pub giving, often pictorially, the name of the pub and details of the brewery which owns it. Some pictorial signs, such as those of Palmer's of Bridport, are works of art, and the 'collecting' of inn signs is a hobby in itself, which can often reveal much of the social, industrial, or feudal history of a locality.

Invert Sugar A form of easily fermentable sugar used in brewing.

Invicta Shepherd Neame's cask best bitter (1044), named after the white horse symbol of Kent.

Irish Ale Breweries Guinness-controlled group with a third stake by Britain's Allied Breweries, running three breweries in Eire: Smithwicks of Kilkenny, Cherrys of Waterford, and Macardles of Dundalk, producing only keg and bottled beers.

Irish Moss A mixture of two marine algae sometimes used to clear beer during brewing.

Irish Red Ale See *Killian*.

Isinglass Another name for *Finings*.

[J]

Jack Pot Hook Norton's bottled best bitter (1036) from Oxfordshire.

Jacobs Small brewery set up in Nailsea, near Bristol, in 1980. Taken over by Halls in 1984, but still producing Jacobs Best Bitter (1038).

Jager Davenport's weak (1032) bottled and canned lager from Birmingham.

James Paine See *Paine*.

Janner's Cask bitter (1038) from the Mill Brewery, Newton Abbot, Devon.

Jenlain The classic Bière de Garde (laying-down beer) of northern France, from the town of Jenlain near Valenciennes. Top-fermented and unpasteurised, it has an alcohol content of 6.5 per cent.

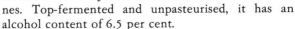

Jennings Traditional brewery in the far northwest of England, in Cockermouth, Cumbria, whose real ales are available not only in all 90 tied houses, but also in a number of Bass pubs in the region. *Cask beers*: Mild (1033), Bitter (1035). *Keg*: Castle Mild (1033), Bitter (1035).

JK King & Barnes sweet bottled stout (1034) from Sussex, named after the brewery's founder, James King (1807–77).

John Arkell Bitter See *Arkell*.

John Brown Hall & Woodhouse's bottled brown ale (1031) from Dorset, and Felinfoel's sweeter brown ale (1032) from South Wales.

John Bull Ind Coope's keg, canned, and bottled bitter (1036) from its Romford brewery. A stronger version is brewed at Burton for export (1053).

John Courage Courage's keg and bottled premium pale ale (1042), named after their founder who started brewing opposite the Tower of London in 1787.

John Devenish Low-gravity cask bitter (1032) from

Devenish in the southwest. Also in one-litre bottles.

John Groves Devenish keg bitter (1034) from Dorset, named after the Weymouth brewery they took over in 1960.

John Marston Keg version of Marston's premium bitter, Pedigree (1043).

John Peel Matthew Brown's premium cask and keg bitter (1040) from Blackburn, named after the trademark of the Workington brewery taken over in 1975 and now used to brew lager. A premium lager (1060) exported to the USA is also called John Peel.

John Thompson Home-brew pub, named after the landlord, at Ingleby, Derbyshire. *Cask beer*: JTS XXX (1045). Sold in the free trade as Lloyd's Country Bitter.

John Young Chairman of London's famous family brewers, who has lent his name to their London Lager (1037).

Jolly Fenman Clifton Inns home-brew pub, Sidcup, Kent. *Cask beers*: Blackfen Bitter (1037), Fenman Fortune (1047).

Jolly Roger Colourful brewery at the Old Anchor, Upton-on-Severn, Worcs. *Cask beers*: Jolly Roger Bitter (1035), Severn Bore (1045), Old Anchor Ale (1060).

Joseph Holt See *Holt*.

Jubilee Bass's bottled sweet stout (1040). Also Hook Norton bottled strong ale (1049) and Mary Ann bottled strong lager (1064).

Jug and Bottle The off-sales part of a pub, usually served via a hatch from the main bar, traditionally where draught beer is served in jugs or bottled beer is bought to be taken home.

Juke Box Originating in US bars, a machine for playing music of a customer's choice on payment of a small sum of money.

[K]

Kaiserdom A Bavarian brewery in Bamberg specialising in the town's famous Rauchbier (smoked beer).

Kaliber Guinness non-alcoholic lager.

Kaltenberg Whitbread's bottled Pils (1047) from Bavaria.

Keeve Scottish term for a bulk barrel (36 gallons).

Keg (1) Short for 'keg beer', pressurised brewery-conditioned or processed beer, usually pasteurised. **(2)** A container for brewery-conditioned beer. Keg beer was first developed by Watneys in the 1930s for export and sale in clubs or hotels which could not handle cask. Flowers first promoted it in the 1950s, and then it really took off in the 1960s with the arrival of the national brewers and their need for an easy-to-handle product which could be sold all over the country – at a premium price.

Keg Buster Cartoon character created by Bill Tidy who epitomises the fighting spirit of the British beer drinker, as seen with the rise of CAMRA, the Campaign for Real Ale.

Kellar Light lager from Arkell of Swindon (1033). The foreign-sounding name is in fact a play on the family name.

Kellerbrau Charles Wells keg and bottled lager (1034) from Bedford.

Kentish Ales Small Kent brewery, formerly the Royal Tunbridge Wells brewery, re-established in 1984. *Cask beers*: Royal Pale (1035), Royal Sovereign (1040), Royal Porter (1050).

Kentish Gold Cask bitter (1035) from Ashford Brewery.

Kestrel Younger's weak keg and canned lager (1032), going cheap.

Kettle Another name for the *Copper*.

Keystone A wooden bung put into the tap hole of a cask. The centre of a keystone is partially bored through, and the tap is driven in through this piece, leaving the outer wooden ring as a 'washer' sealing the tap into the cask.

Kieselguhr A mineral powder used in some breweries to filter beer.

Kilderkin An 18-gallon cask, known as a 'kil' or a 'kiln'.

Killian George Killian's Irish Red Ale is brewed both by Coors of America and Pelforth of France (as Bière Rousse). This beer full of blarney is produced under licence from Letts of Eire – who ceased brewing themselves in 1956!

Kilning The final stage in the malting process: barley is placed into kilns at high temperatures in order to halt germination. Also known as 'curing'. Hops are dried in the well-known kilns called Oast Houses.

Kimberley Ales Beers produced by Hardys & Hansons of Nottingham.

Kindl One of West Berlin's two major breweries, famous for its white beer. See *Berliner Weisse*.

King & Barnes Traditional Sussex family brewery, with real ale in all 58 pubs, which in recent years has built a new brewhouse at Horsham. About to introduce lager. *Cask beers*: Sussex Mild (1034), Sussex Bitter (1034), Old Ale (1046), Draught Festive (1050). *Bottled*: Brown Ale (1034), Sussex Bitter (1034), JK Stout (1034), Old Ale (1046), Festive Ale (1050), Golding Ale (1075).

Kingfisher Perhaps the best-known beer from India.

King Keg Greene King's keg bitter (1038) from East Anglia.

King's Ale Matthew Brown's strong bottled ale (1060) from Blackburn.

King's Arms Home-brew pub, Bishop Auckland, County Durham. *Cask beer*: Weardale Bitter (1038).

Kingsdown Arkell's strong ale (1050) from their Kingsdown Brewery, Swindon, available on draught and in bottle.

King's Wood Keg best bitter (1039) from New Forest, Hampshire.

Kinross Bottled 'Scotch' ale (1064) which has never seen life north of the border, being brewed for export by Paines of Cambridgeshire.

Kirin The giant of Japanese brewing and the second largest brewery in the world, best known for its lager (4.5 per cent alcohol) but also producing a rarer stout.

KK Greene King's cask light mild (1031) from East Anglia.

Kolsch Cologne's very own top-fermented German beer style, of medium strength, soft taste, and pale colour. Only a dozen breweries in Cologne are allowed to use the name. The best-known is Kuppers.

KPA Brakspear's Keg Pale Ale (1035) from Henley-on-Thames. A brewery-conditioned version of the cask bitter, but unlike Beehive not pressurised in the container.

Krausen The process of adding a portion of vigorously fermenting wort from primary fermentation to 'green' beer as a means of inducing natural conditioning. Also used as an alternative to priming.

Kriek A Belgian Gueuze beer in which the second fermentation has been caused by adding cherries.

Kronen The oldest Dortmund brewery and the most popular in the German city itself, producing the fine Dortmunder, Kronen Export (5.2 per cent alcohol), and the weaker award-winning Classic.

Kronenbourg Giant French brewery from Strasbourg which lends its name to Britain's leading premium keg lager, Kronenbourg 1664 (1046), brewed in Britain by Harp and Courage.

Krystal Lite Burtonwood's low-calorie bottled and keg beer (1030) from Cheshire.

Kulminator The strongest regularly-produced beer in the world. This German Eisbock – full name Kulminator 28 Urtyp Hell – is lagered for nine months by the Bavarian EKU brewery near Bayreuth, and frozen to increase its strength by the removal of water ice, giving it a horrific alcohol content of 12.4 per cent.

Kuppers The most widely exported brand of Kolsch (4.5 per cent alcohol), the unique light ale of Köln (German for Cologne).

[L]

Labatt One of Canada's 'Big Three' brewing groups, based in Ontario, with the best-selling brand 'Blue', a sweet Pilsener. Also brews Skol, Budweiser, and an unsuccessful Guinness under licence.

Labologist A collector of beer bottle labels. A labologists' society started in 1959 after a Guinness promotion encouraged the hobby.

Lager Beer fermented with the 'bottom-fermentation' yeast *Saccharomyces uvarum* (formerly *S. carlsbergensis*). Production of lager differs from ale in several other respects: lower modified malts are used in the decoction rather than the infusion mash system; the liquor is generally soft and low in mineral salts; Continental, seedless, low alpha acid hops are used (eg Saaz or Hallertau); primary fermentation is at a lower temperature than for ale, and secondary fermentation in closed conditioning tanks takes place at around 0°C for a lengthy period, often exceeding four weeks. Few British-brewed lagers conform to European practices, despite their European names. They are of lower gravity than their European equivalents. European lagers are often not pasteurised or filtered, but merely racked bright off the dormant yeast at the end of fermentation, and are then dispensed from the cask under the pressure generated by their natural conditioning. British lagers are normally filtered, pasteurised, recarbonated, and dispensed under CO_2 pressure from kegs via flash coolers. Because it is normally served at low temperatures (around 46°F), lager needs to be of higher gravity and body to have any flavour; weak British lagers tend to be low in gravity, body, and flavour.

Lambic The strange 'wild' beers of Belgium. Wild yeasts from the air ferment these wheat brews from the Senne Valley, west of Brussels, giving them a unique sour taste and an alcohol content of 4.5 per cent. Lambic is usually blended to form Gueuze, and other variations are Faro (sweetened), Kriek (cherry), and

Framboise (raspberry).

Lamot Belgian brewery whose bottled Pils (1045) is imported by Bass.

Lancer Strong bottled lager from Harp in Eire.

Landlord One of the great bitter beers of Britain (1042), from Timothy Taylor of Yorkshire, named, of course, after the popular name for a pub keeper.

Landsdorf Hardington's filtered but not pasteurised draught lager (1034) from Somerset.

Lass O'Gowrie Whitbread home-brew pub (using malt extract) , Manchester. *Cask beers*: Bitter (1035), Strong (1045).

Lates Slang term for drinks sold after permitted hours of opening.

La Trappe The only Dutch Trappist ale (6.5 per cent alcohol), from the Schaapskooi abbey brewery.

Lauter Tun A vessel which holds the mash and separates wort from spent grain. Usually found in decoction mash systems, which use a mash mixing vessel, a mash cooking vessel (mash copper or cereal cooker), a lauter tun or mash separator, and a wort copper; can also be used for infusion mashing. Many lauter tuns incorporate rotating knives or blades to keep the bottom of the mash open and give a fast run-off of wort, and one 'strainmaster' system (patented by Anheuser-Busch Inc) incorporates internal stainless steel perforated straining tubes for run-off of wort.

LB Burt's light bitter (1030) from Ventnor, Isle of Wight, rarely found unpressurised.

LBA Guernsey Brewery's draught mild (1037.7). The initials stand for London Brewery Ale, the name of the Channel Island company until the turn of the century.

Lees One of Manchester's surviving independent family breweries, with 129 pubs in the north of the city and North Wales. *Cask beers*: GB Mild (1032), Bitter (1038), Moonraker (1074). *Keg*: Mild (1032), Bitter (1038), Lees Lager (1034), Edelbrau (1052). *Bottled*: Light Ale (1030), Brown Ale (1033), Export (1054), Archer Stout (1042), Moonraker (1074), Tulip Lager (1034), Edelbrau (1052), Edelbrau Diät Pils (1048).

Leicester Brewery New clubs brewery set up in

Syston, Leics, in 1983, producing only keg beers: Old John (1036), Sport Lager (1036).

Leith See *Argyle*.

Leopard The smallest of New Zealand's three brewing groups, but ironically the best-known since it has emphasised exports. Jointly owned by Heineken and Malayan Breweries.

Letts This Irish brewing company at Enniscorthy, County Wexford, stopped production in 1956 – but still licenses Pelforth of France and Coors of America to brew its former Ruby Ale as George Killian's Bière Rousse or Irish Red Ale.

Leyland Tiny brewery (using malt extract) in the Brewing Up shop, Leyland, Lancs. *Cask beer*: Tiger Ale (1038).

Licensing Justices A body of up to 15 ordinary lay magistrates who sit on local licensing committees, dealing with licence applications and renewals.

Liddington East Midlands beer wholesalers who in 1984 took over one of the pioneers of the new brewery movement, Litchborough, founded in 1974, and moved the plant to their Rugby depot. *Cask beers*: Litchborough Bitter (1036), Tudor Ale (1044).

Liefmans Belgian brewery (surprisingly owned by Vaux of Sunderland) based in Oudenaarde, a town famous for its top-fermenting brown ales. Liefmans produce the best in huge litre bottles, notably Goudenband Speciaal Provisie.

Light Ale A low-gravity (hence light in body, not necessarily light in colour) bottled ale, usually of less strength than 'ordinary' bitter, though of higher condition and lower hoppiness. A Scottish 'light' or 60/- ale is normally a dark-coloured draught beer of around 1030–1035 OG, not unlike an English mild.

Light Oxford Morrell's bottled light ale (1032) from Oxford.

Lindemans Belgian farmhouse brewery at Vlezenbeek producing wild Lambic beers, which are now exported to France and the USA.

Lindener Gilde-brau Bottled Diät Pils (1050) imported from Hanover by Thwaites of Blackburn.

Lion Ales Matthew Brown's beers from Blackburn, notably Lion Mild (1031) and Lion Bitter (1036). Camerons of Hartlepool also brew a cask Lion Bitter (1036), and the name is in addition given to Banks's keg mild (1035) and bitter (1037) from Wolverhampton. Morrell's of Oxford also use a lion trademark and, abroad, Lion Beers are the biggest brewing group in New Zealand. Even Lowenbrau means lion beer!

Liqueur Castletown's bottled barley wine (1072) from the Isle of Man.

Liquor The brewer's name for the water used to make beer. In a brewery, water is only 'water' when it is used for lesser tasks like washing or cooling.

Litchborough See *Liddington*.

Little John Bottled strong ale (1070) from Home of Nottingham, of course.

Lloyd See *John Thompson*.

Lloyd & Trouncer Ansells subsidiary company in North Wales, running some 180 pubs and extensive free trade. Set up in 1981, and named after two former breweries, Lloyds of Newport and Trouncer of Shrewsbury.

Loburg Stella Artois bottled lager (1051) from Belgium.

Local Popular name for a neighbourhood pub with local trade, or the name for a pub regularly used by a person ('My local is . . .'). Also the name for bitters from Greenall Whitley (1038), Shipstone (1037), Randall Vautier (1036), and Tisbury (1037).

Local Line Chudley's cask bitter (1038) from London.

London Lager Young's keg and bottled lager (1037); named in full John Young's London Lager, after the brewery chairman, John Young.

London Pride Fuller's fine best bitter (1041.5) from Chiswick, which is stronger in bottle (1045) than on draught.

London Stout A name now chiefly used by breweries outside Britain, like Moosehead of Canada.

Lone Star Famous Texas brewery and beer from San Antonio, owned by Olympia of Washington.

Long Life Allied's 'beer brewed for the can' (1040)

from Wrexham. Also in keg. Export version is stronger (1046).

Longman Alice Brewery keg lager (1040) from Inverness.

Long Pull Serving over-measure, as for example a generous 'half' into a pint glass. This is a specific offence under the Licensing Act, whereas serving short measure is not (it is dealt with under weights and measures legislation).

Loose Head See *Head*.

Lord's Strong ale (1048) from Chudley of London, named after the cricket ground.

Lorimer & Clark Classic traditional Scottish brewery in Edinburgh, taken over by Vaux of Sunderland in 1946 but still brewing a wide range of fine cask beers, though its Scottish tied estate was sold to Allied Breweries. The 70/- is sold as Lorimer's Best Scotch in Vaux houses. *Cask beers*: 60/- (1030.5), 70/- or Best Scotch (1036), 80/- (1043), Caledonian Strong (1077). *Keg*: Best Scotch (1036). *Bottled*: Export (1044), Barley Wine (1074).

Lounge A pub room which is more comfortably furnished than the public bar, and where drink prices, as a consequence, are higher.

Low C Marston's bottled and keg low carbohydrate ale (1030), advertised as 'for beer drinkers with a weight problem'.

Lowenbrau The world-famous Lion brewery of Munich which licenses Allied Breweries in Britain and Miller in the United States to produce pale imitations of German beer. In Britain, keg Lowenbrau (1041) is brewed in Wrexham; the bottled Pils (1047) and Special Export (1051) are imported.

Lumley Old Ale Dark winter brew (1050) from Hermitage, West Sussex.

Luncheon Ale Light bottled 'dinner' or 'luncheon' ales were once produced by most breweries. Only Home of Nottingham still retain the name (1034).

Lupulin The sticky yellow powder in the hop cone which gives the hop its bittering and preserving power.

LVA Licensed Victuallers Association – a voluntary society of landlords devoted to preserving their interests and the interests of 'the trade'. LVAs are arranged roughly on licensing districts. Complimentary to the LVA is the 'auxiliary', an association of publicans' wives primarily devoted to charitable and social activities.

[M]

MA Brains beer especially produced for The Crown, Skewen, near Swansea – a brewery mix of SA and Dark.

M&B See *Mitchells & Butlers*.

Macardles Dundalk brewery producing keg and bottled ales for eastern Eire. Part of the Guinness-controlled Irish Ale Breweries.

McEwan The 'Cavalier' half of Scottish Brewers. See *Scottish & Newcastle*.

McEwan-Younger Scottish & Newcastle's Northwest England, Yorkshire, and North Wales marketing company.

Mackeson Britain's best-known bottled sweet stout (1042), from Whitbread.

Maclay One of only two remaining Scottish independent breweries left after the takeover typhoon hit the country, supplying fine ales from its Alloa brewery to its 25 pubs. *Cask beers*: 60/- Light (1030), 70/- Heavy (1035), 80/- Export (1040). *Keg*: As cask. *Bottled*: Imperial Pale (1030), Stout (1032), Export (1040), Strong Ale (1060).

McMullen Hertford family brewery since 1827 which recently built a new brewhouse. Serves real ale in many of its 157 pubs. *Cask beers*: AK Mild (1033), Country Bitter (1041), Christmas Ale (1070). *Keg*: Mac's No.1 (1036), Hartsman Lager (1035), Steingold (1042).

Bottled: Mac's Brown (1031), Mac's No.1 (1036), Castle (1047), Olde Time (1070), Farmer's Ale (1036) – litre bottles only.

Mac's Beers from McMullen of Hertford, especially keg and bottled No.1 (1036) and bottled brown (1031).

Maes A Belgian brewery owned by Watneys, well-known for its Pils. Also brews an Abbaye-style beer called Grimbergen.

Magnet The sign of John Smith's of Tadcaster, and the name of their premium keg bitter (1040) and bottled Pale (1042) and Old (1070).

Maiden Oak New brewery set up in Londonderry, Northern Ireland, in 1985.

Maidstone Ale Goacher's best bitter (1040), Maidstone, Kent. Also Maidstone Light (1036).

Malt Barley which has been partially germinated and then kilned to convert the starch into fermentable sugars, so providing the majority of the carbohydrate material that is fermented by yeast into alcohol. Malt also gives body and flavour to beer and adds to its colour. Malt is often known as 'the soul of beer'.

Malt Extract If the wort extracted from the mash is boiled under a very low pressure, most of the water content can be evaporated off, leaving a treacly syrup containing the sugars extracted from the malt. Specialised companies produce malt extract, mostly for home-brew kits, but many brewers also use extract to supplement or modify their mash and some pub breweries avoid the expense of installing a mash tun by using only extract, made up with water, put directly into the copper.

Malthouse Low-gravity keg and canned beer (1033) from Hall & Woodhouse of Dorset.

Maltings A place where raw barley is converted into malt by the maltster.

Malt Liquor An American beer style in which strong unhopped lagers are fermented out to produce a thin but potent drink. Popular in run-down inner city areas in the USA where the need to get drunk comes first. The major British brands are Colt 45 and Breaker.

Malton Small brewery behind the Crown Hotel,

Malton, North Yorkshire, set up in this once famous brewing town in 1985. *Cask beer*: Double Chance (1039).

Malt Shovel A wooden shovel used to turn over germinating barley at floor maltings.

Maltster A trained official responsible for overseeing the malting process in a maltings. Similar to the head brewer in a brewery.

Malt Stout Another popular name for bottled stout, still used by Morrell's of Oxford (1042).

Malt Syrup A concentrated malt extract used in the mash to help convert grain or adjuncts, or in the copper (when it is called 'copper syrup') to extend brew length or adjust gravity.

Malt Tax The way the Government took its whack from beer until 1880, when beer duty was introduced.

Manns Watney's East Midlands company based in Northampton, with 800 pubs. One of the oddest of the revived brewery names, since Manns was a London brewery, famous for its brown ale. The Northampton brewery taken over by Watney was Phipps! All beers are now brewed in London or Manchester. *Cask*: Manns IPA (1038), Bitter (1040). *Keg*: Triple Crown (1033), Mild (1034), Draught (1036), Best Bitter (1040). *Bottled*: Light Ale (1034), Brown Ale (1034), Export Pale (1048).

Mansfield East Midlands brewery with some 200 pubs, which began brewing real ale again in 1982, though it is only available in a minority of pubs. Took over North Country Breweries of Hull in 1985. *Cask beer*: 4XXXX (1045). *Keg*: Mild (1035), Bitter (1039), Marksman Lager (1039). *Bottled*: Pale Ale (1034).

Manx Pure Beer Act Germany is not the only country to protect the purity of its beers (see *Reinheitsgebot*). The Isle of Man also decrees that its ales shall be brewed only from malt, hops, and sugar. Castletown and Okell still observe the 1874 Act.

Maple Leaf Ind Coope home-brew pub at Newark, Notts. *Cask beer*: Bitter (1037).

Ma Pardoes Famous Black Country home-brew house at Netherton, near Dudley. More correctly known as the Old Swan. Bought with the help of CAMRA in 1985 to safeguard this unique pub. *Cask beer*: Bitter (1034).

Marcher Lager (1034) specially brewed by Marstons for their Border subsidiary in North Wales.

Maris Otter Strain of barley regarded as the best quality for ale malt, grown in England and Wales.

Marisco Tavern Home-brew pub (using malt extract) on Lundy Island in the Bristol Channel, appropriately brewing Puffin Bitter (1040).

Market Small brewery in the Market Porter pub, Southwark, London. *Cask beer*: Beach's Borough Bitter (1038).

Market Extension An extension to normal permitted licensing hours made under an order of general exception that allows certain pubs to open later on market days. Particularly common in market towns in northern England.

Marksman Mansfield's keg lager (1039).

Marston Major regional brewery with 700 pubs stretching from Cumbria to Hampshire, all supplied from their Burton brewery, notably with the famous Pedigree. In 1984 they tarnished their traditional image by taking over Border of Wrexham and closing down the brewery. *Cask beers*: Capital (1030), Mercian Mild (1032), Burton Bitter (1037), Pedigree (1043), Merrie Monk (1043), Owd Rodger (1080). *Keg*: Albion Mild (1030), Low C (1030), Albion Bitter (1037), Burton Bitter (1037), John Marston (1043), Pilsner Lager (1038). *Bottled*: Low C (1030), Light Ale (1032), Pedigree (1046), Owd Rodger (1080). See also *Border*.

Marston Moor Small brewery near York set up in 1984. *Cask beer*: Cromwell Bitter (1037).

Martin Small brewery at Martin, near Dover, producing cask Martin Ale (1040), since 1984.

Martin's Pale Ale This Courage beer (1068), known in England as Bulldog, is bottled in Antwerp by the John Martin company for sale in Belgium, where English strong pale ales are a speciality. Even Bass is brewed to a higher gravity for Belgium.

Mary Ann See *Ann Street*.

Marzen A full-bodied (5.5 per cent alcohol) copper-coloured lager originating in Vienna but developed in Munich as their stronger Marzen (March) brews which were fermented over the summer for drinking at the Oktoberfest.

Mash The infusion that extracts the fermentable materials from the malt. The mash tun is filled to a depth of several feet with grist (milled malt), and then hot liquor (water) is run in to form a porridge-like mass. The mixture is left to steep. During the mash enzymes in the malt, activated by the hot water, convert the starches into sugars and these sugars pass into the liquid. After several hours the liquid, which is now the sweet wort, is run off, and the spent grains are emptied to be sold off as cattle food. See also *Decoction* and *Infusion*.

Mash Tun The vessel in which the mash is infused. The mash tun has a squat cylindrical shape, surrounded with considerable insulation to allow the mash temperature to be maintained. The vessel has a false floor of perforated plates which retain the grains as the wort is run off.

Master Ale Holden's powerful bottled old ale (1080) from the Black Country.

Master Brew General brand name for Shepherd Neame's dark cask mild (1031), bitter (1036), and keg light mild XX (1033) from Kent.

Mather The chief producers of Black Beer. The original Leeds company is now owned by the Matthew Clark wines and spirits group. Bass also have a stake. See *Black Beer*.

Matthew Brown See *Brown*.

Matty's Light Matthew Brown's light keg beer (1033) from Blackburn, primarily brewed for Cumbria.

Maturation The storage of beer for a period during which its quality improves as it matures and as impurities settle out.

Mauldon Small family brewery in Sudbury, Suffolk, revived in 1982. *Cask beers*: Mauldon's Bitter (1037), Special (1044), Christmas Reserve (1065).

Medallion Federation keg lager (1036) from Newcastle.

Medium Irish term for a half-pint of draught Guinness.

Megakeggery Derogatory term for the huge processed-beer factories built by the national brewers.

Meister The Pils brand from Germany's largest brewery, Dortmunder Actien.

Melbourn Lincolnshire company with 38 pubs. No longer brewing. The Stamford brewery is now a museum. Beers from Samuel Smith.

Mellow Elgood's keg mild (1032) from Wisbech in the Fens.

Mercian Marston's cask dark mild (1032) from Burton-upon-Trent.

Merlin Usher's light cask ale (1032) for South Wales.

Merrie Monk Darker version of Marston's Pedigree (1043), claimed to be the strongest mild in Britain.

Michelob Anheuser-Busch's premium American beer, with a higher gravity than its St Louis stable-mate, Budweiser.

Midlands Mild John Smith's stronger keg mild (1036), specially brewed for the West Midlands.

Mild An ale of low gravity and hop rate, hence rounder, usually slightly sweeter, and distinctly less bitter on the palate and in aroma than more highly hopped bitters. Mild is usually (but not always) darker in colour than bitter, through use of a higher-roast malt or caramel. There are considerable variations in mild styles, from the 'classic' milds such as Thwaites Best Mild or Ansells, to lighter-coloured milds such as Banks's or Greene King KK, to stronger heavy milds such as Marston's Merrie Monk.

Milk Stout Once a popular name for sweet stouts until leaned on by stricter product description laws. Only Guernsey Brewery's bottled Milk Stout (1042) survives, out of reach of mainland legislation.

Mill Small Devon brewery set up in Newton Abbot in 1983. *Cask beers*: Janner's Ale (1038), Devon Special (1043).

Miller American beer giant, second only to Anheuser-Busch, from the US brewing capital of Milwaukee, Wisconsin. Once famous for its 'High Life' lager, Miller is now known for popularising light beers. Also brew a poor imitation of German Lowenbrau. Owned by Philip Morris, the tobacco giants.

Minera Small brewery run by Lloyd & Trouncer in North Wales at the City Arms, Minera, Wrexham. *Cask beer*: Minera Bitter (1037).

Miners Arms First of the new wave of home-brew houses in 1973, producing bottle-conditioned beer, which in 1981 moved site to Westbury-sub-Mendip, Somerset, to brew draught beer for the free trade. Also famous for its 'snails and ales' as it provides snails for eating. *Cask beer*: Own Ale (1040).

Mitchells Lancaster's surviving family brewery with 51 pubs, which in 1985 closed its city centre site and moved to Yates & Jackson's former brewery, after its Lancaster rivals had been taken over and closed down by Thwaites of Blackburn. *Cask beers*: Mild (1034), Bitter (1036), ESB (1044.8). *Keg*: As cask. *Bottled*: Brown Ale (1034), Bitter Ale (1036), ESB (1044.8), Centenary (1080).

Mitchells & Butlers Bass's Birmingham brewery, with 1,700 pubs, which dominates England's second largest city. Also runs two other West Midlands breweries in Walsall (Highgate) and Wolverhampton (Springfield). *Cask beers*: Mild (1035), Brew XI (1040). *Keg*: As cask, plus DPA (1033). *Bottled*: Light (1032), Sam Brown (1035), Allbright (1040), Export (1048).

Modification The germination stage of the malting process (after steeping), when the barley starts to sprout shoots and the chemical actions begin.

Moles Small Wiltshire brewery set up in Melksham in 1982. Takes its name from the brewer's nickname. *Cask beers*:

Mole's Bitter (1040), Mole's 97 (1048).

Molson The largest of Canada's 'Big Three' breweries, based in Quebec, producing a hoppier range of beers than Carling or Labatt.

Monarch Morland's strong bottled ale (1065) from Abingdon. Formerly the name of their barley wine, which was discontinued.

Monk Export Northern Ireland name for canned McEwan's Export (1042).

Monkscroft House Ale A 'take-off' of Traquair House Ale, produced by Belhaven of Scotland for export to Italy, right down to the similar label. The bottled ale (1070) is a pale version of Belhaven's strong ale, Fowler's Wee Heavy.

Monmouth Small brewery at the Queen's Head, Monmouth, Wales. *Cask beers*: Ten Thirty Five (1035), Piston (1045).

Moonraker Odd how tales get around. Lees of Manchester claim their heavenly strong cask and bottled ale (1074) got its name from locals trying to rake the reflection of the moon off a pond. Gibbs Mew of Salisbury claim the same for their bottled brown ale (1032) – only their lads were really raking in barrels of smuggled beer beneath the surface.

Moorhouses Established producer of hop bitters in Burnley, which in 1979 began brewing beer, and two years later was taken over by the Hutchinson leisure group. In 1985 taken over by Apollo Leisure of Oxford. *Cask beers*: Premier Bitter (1036), Pendle Witches Brew (1050). *Bottled*: Premier (1036).

Moosehead This Canadian brewery has become a cult in the United States, where its name and frontier setting in Nova Scotia and New Brunswick boost the appeal of its bolder range of beers.

Moravia A dry, hoppy bottled Pils (4.9 per cent alcohol) from the Holsten group of North Germany, brewed in Lüneburg.

Morland Britain's second oldest independent brewery, dating back to 1711, with 215 pubs in the Thames Valley around Abingdon, Oxfordshire. *Cask beers*: Mild (1032), Bitter (1035), Best Bitter (1042). *Keg*: Artists (1032). *Bottled*: Brown (1032), Light (1032), Viking Pale (1042), Old Speckled Hen (1050), Monarch (1065).

Morning Advertiser A daily newspaper for publicans.

Morrell Oxford's only remaining in-dependent brewery produces a fine range of real ales for its 140 pubs. *Cask beers*: Light (1032), Dark Mild (1032.6), Bitter (1036), Varsity (1041), Celebra-tion (1066), College (1073). *Keg*: Pale (1032), Friars Ale (1036), Varsity (1041). *Bottled*: Light Oxford (1032), Brown Oxford (1032), Castle Ale (1041), Malt Stout (1042), Celebra-tion (1066), College Ale (1073).

Mort Subite The extravagantly named 'sudden death' which, despite jokes like 'from beer to bier', is no stronger than other Belgian Lambic beers.

Mother-in-Law Rude term for a pint of stout and bitter.

Mr Cherrys Sea-front home-brew pub in St Leonards, Sussex. *Cask beers*: Hastings (1042), Conqueror (1066).

MSB Mak's Special Beer (1050), brewed for Mak's Bar, Penzance, Cornwall, which takes the bulk of produc-tion from the tiny Pensans Brewery.

Mug Popular name given to a beer glass with a handle.

Münchner The dark, malty, bottom-fermenting beers originating in Munich, which are now more often found in their pale (Helles) form. Has fairly low strength for German beer of around 4 per cent alcohol.

Murphy Irish stout brewers of Cork, now owned by Heineken of the Netherlands.

[N]

NALHM National Association of Licensed House Managers. The pub and club managers' trade union.

Naturally-conditioned Beer which continues to mature in the cask or bottle.

Near Beer Sober Switzerland can lay claim to having created one beer style – alcohol-free lager. Brands like Birell and Ex-Beer are now sold throughout Europe, while Britain weighs in with Barbican.

New Fermor Arms Home-brew pub, Rufford, Lancs. *Cask beer*: Blezards Bitter (1039).

New Forest Hampshire brewery at Cadnam set up in 1980 by a soft drinks firm, chiefly to supply the Southampton club trade with keg beer. *Cask beer*: New Forest Real Ale (1036). *Keg*: CB (1031), Woodsman Mild (1034), New Forest (1036), King's Wood (1039), Forest Lager (1038).

Newcastle Tyneside arm of Scottish & Newcastle, particularly known for its unusual strong 'Broon' ale, running 690 pubs in Northeast England. *Cask beer*: Exhibition (1042). *Keg*: IPA (1032), Bitter (1036), Exhibition (1042). *Bottled*: Amber (1033), Brown Ale (1045).

New Inn Tetley home-brew pub, Harrogate, Yorks. *Cask beer*: Gate Ale (1045).

Newman First American 'new wave' brewery to introduce naturally-conditioned draught beer, Newman's Pale Ale, in the USA. Set up in Albany, New York, in 1981.

Newton & Ridley Coronation Street's famous brewers, who sadly don't exist beyond the TV set of the Rover's Return.

Newton's Ale Devenish keg bitter (1032) for the southwest club trade. Also Wilson's keg bitter (1032).

97 Mole's special cask bitter (1048) from Wiltshire. Named after the gyle number of the first brew.

90/- Ales Scottish term for strong ales. See *Shilling*

System.

Nip A third of a pint; a common size for bottles of barley wine or very strong ale.

Noggin Charles Wells keg best bitter (1039) from Bedford, which once featured a huge wooden capstan on the bar.

Norfolk Pride Woodforde's cask bitter (1036) from Norfolk. Also Norfolk Porter (1041).

Norseman Vaux of Sunderland's former 'Viking' keg lager, now replaced by Tuborg on draught, and only available in can (1032).

North Country Hull Brewery was acquired by Northern Foods in 1972 and renamed North Country Breweries, reflecting further takeover ambitions which failed to materialise. In 1985 taken over by Mansfield Brewery. Mainly sells bright beers under the misleading Old Tradition name, but in 1982 did introduce a cask beer for its 210 pubs. *Cask beer*: Riding Bitter (1038). *Keg*: Old Tradition Mild (1033), Bitter (1038), Anchor Export (1048), Hopfenperle Lager (1038).

North Eastern Bass keg bitter (1032) for the north-east.

North Star Arkell's keg bitter (1036) from the railway town of Swindon, named after an early steam locomotive.

Northern Clubs See *Federation*.

Northerner Timothy Taylor's bottled dark ale (1033) from Yorkshire.

Northgate Wadworth's keg bitter (1036) named after their Northgate Brewery in Devizes, which was built in 1885 on the site of the Wiltshire town's old north gate, still used as the brewery symbol.

Norwich Watney's East Anglian company which saw the inevitable rocky end of the takeover trail in 1985 when Watneys, having absorbed the bulk of Norfolk's pubs in the 1960s, closed the final Norwich brewery. The future of these local beers is now uncertain, though some will be brewed in London or Manchester. *Cask beers*: S&P Bitter (1038), Bullards Old (1057). *Keg*: Norwich Mild (1032), Bitter (1036), Anchor Bitter (1034), Anglian Strong (1048). *Bottled*: Brown Ale (1032), Light

Ale (1032), Pale (1036), Anglian Strong (1048).

Nourishing Stout Stouts were often credited with being good for you; hence 'My goodness my Guinness'. The name survives with Gales bottled stout (1034) from Hampshire, and Sam Smith's (1050) from Yorkshire.

NULV National Union of Licensed Victuallers. The pub tenants' national organisation, acting as an umbrella for local LVAs.

No. 1 McMullen's keg and bottled pale ale (1036); Okell's bottled barley wine (1070); and Selby's naturally-conditioned bottled ale (1039).

No. 3 Younger's distinctive dark cask ale (1043) from Edinburgh.

No. 9 Premium cask bitter (1043) from the Bodicote Brewery, near Banbury, Oxon.

Nut Brown Popular name for bottled brown ales like Adnams, Gales, and Shipstones.

[O]

Oak Small Cheshire brewery set up in 1982 in Ellesmere Port. *Cask beers*: Best Bitter (1038), Old Oak (1044), Porter (1050), Double Dagger (1050).
Oakhill Small brewery near Bath first set up in 1981 as Beacon Brewery and revived in 1984 under new name. Set in old Oakhill Brewery buildings. *Cask beers*: Farmer's Ale (1038), Oakhill Stout (1045). *Keg*: Oakhill Lager (1033).

Oast House Popular name for a hop kiln. Their distinctive cowled roofs make them a prominent feature of the Kent countryside.

OB Beers from Oldham Brewery of Manchester; the initials are usually printed on the side of a bell.

OBB Old Brewery Bitter (1038.9) from Sam Smiths of Tadcaster.

Occasional Permissions A licence to sell liquor

(usually at an outside bar) for up to 24 hours, made to anyone over 18 years who is an accredited representative of a non-profit-making organisation. Four such licences may be granted each year (Occasional Permissions Act, 1983).

OG See *Original Gravity*.

Okell Larger of the two independent breweries on the Isle of Man, brewing 'Falcon Ales' from its fine Douglas brewery for 71 pubs. *Cask beers*: Mild (1035), Bitter (1036). *Keg*: As cask. *Bottled*: Nut Brown (1035), Pale Ale (1035), No. 1 Barley Wine (1070).

Oktoberfest The great Munich beer festival where vast amounts of Marzenbier are traditionally drunk out of one-litre stoneware steins in huge brewery 'tents'. A rival fair is held in Stuttgart.

Old Ale Now virtually synonymous with 'winter ale', most 'old ales' (eg Adnams, Tolly Cobbold) are produced and sold for only a limited period of the year, usually between November and the end of February. Usually a rich, dark, high-gravity draught ale of considerable body.

Old Anchor Strong cask ale (1060) from the Jolly Roger brewery, Old Anchor Inn, Upton-on-Severn, Worcs.

Old Bank Street Manchester home-brew bar (using malt extract). *Cask beer*: Old Bank St Bitter (1043).

Old Bedford Charles Wells bottled barley wine (1078).

Old Bob Ridley's strong bottled pale ale (1050) from Essex.

Old Bosham Cask bitter (1044) from the Bosham Brewery, West Sussex.

Old Brewery Cask and keg bitter (1038.9) from Yorkshire's oldest brewery, Sam Smith of Tadcaster. Name also used for their bottled strong brown and pale ales.

Old Buzzard Dark winter brew (1048) from Cotleigh, Somerset.

Old Chester Greenall Whitley's strong bottled dark

ale (1067) from Warrington, which is exported under a variety of names including Ebony, Chester Brown, and Warrington Brown. See also *Old Glory*.

Old Dan Daniel Thwaites powerful bottled ale (1075) from Blackburn.

Olde English 800 The strongest beer brewed in the United States (7.5 per cent alcohol), by Blitz-Weinhard of Portland, Oregon.

Olde Time McMullen's bottled strong ale (1070) from Hertford.

Old Expensive Tongue-in-wallet name for strong winter ale (1065) from Burton Bridge, Burton-upon-Trent.

Old Genie Big Lamp draught strong ale (1070) from Newcastle-on-Tyne. Also naturally conditioned in bottle.

Old Glory Greenall Whitley's powerful bottled pale ale (1074) from Warrington, exported as Chester Gold or Old Chester Gold.

Old Gold Premium cask beer (1047) from Ashford Brewery, Kent.

Old Grumble Tisbury strong cask, keg, and bottled ale (1060) from Wiltshire.

Oldham Manchester brewery taken over in 1982 by neighbours, Boddingtons, famous for its OB Pale Ale. Slowly increasing the number of its 87 pubs serving its own real ales. *Cask beers*: Mild (1031.7), Bitter (1037.2). *Keg*: Same as cask (also in tank). *Bottled*: Pale Ale (1037), Old Tom (1065).

Old Hookey Hook Norton's draught strong ale (1049) from Oxfordshire. The bitter is sometimes called 'Young Hookey'.

Old Horizontal Stock's strong ale (1054) from Doncaster.

Old Jock Broughton's strong bottled ale (1070) from Scotland.

Old John Keg bitter (1036) from the Leicester Brewery.

Old Master Raven strong ale (1060) from Brighton.

Old Mill Small brewery set up in Snaith, Humberside, in 1983 by a former Wilson's Brewery production director. *Cask beer*: Traditional Bitter (1037). *Keg*: Bitter (1037).

Old Nick Devil of a bottled barley wine (1084) from Young of London.

Old Nigel Strong winter ale (1060) from Hoskins of Leicester.

Old Norfolk Woodforde's winter ale (1043) from Norfolk.

Old Oak Cask ale (1044) from Oak Brewery, Cheshire.

Old Original The only beer (1050) regularly brewed by Everards on their new plant in Leicester.

Old Peculier Theakston's notorious Yorkshire strong ale (1058.5), named after the Peculier of Masham, the town's ancient ecclesiastical court. Hence the peculiar spelling. OP exported to the Netherlands is even more peculiar, as it has a gravity of 1066. Only OP and XB are now brewed at Theakston's original Masham brewery.

Old Snowy Alexandra's cask winter ale (1054) from Brighton.

Old Speckled Hen Perhaps Britain's oddest beer name. This bottled strong ale (1050) from Morlands was originally brewed to celebrate the 50th anniversary of MG cars in Abingdon in 1979, and has continued driving the curious round the bend ever since. 'Old Speckled Hen' was the nickname given to an early MG car with a mottled, fabric-covered body.

Old Strong A draught winter warmer (1046) from Tolly Cobbold of Ipswich.

Old Swan (1) See *Ma Pardoes*. **(2)** Whitbread home-brew pub (using malt extract) in Cheltenham. *Cask beer*: Bitter (1038).

Old Thumper Ringwood's powerful cask and bottled beer (1060) from Hampshire.

Old Timer Wadworth's famous strong draught ale (1055) from Wiltshire, also available in bottles and cans at the lower gravity of 1052.

Old Tom Famous draught and bottled winter ale (1080) from Robinson of Stockport – named after the brewery cat. Also strong bottled ale (1065) from fellow Manchester brewers, Oldham, and John Smith's keg (1037) for the East Midlands.

Old Tradition Misleading name for filtered mild (1033) and bitter (1038) from North Country Breweries of Hull, served from kegs or tanks.

Olympia Very clean, light American beer from Olympia, Washington – which promotes itself with the remarkably honest slogan: 'It's the water'.

Opening Times The most common licensing hours in England and Wales are 10.30a.m.–2.30p.m. and 5.30–10.30p.m. (11p.m. Friday and Saturday). Sunday 12a.m.–2p.m. and 7–10.30p.m. The weekday limit is 9 or 9½ hours a day with a minimum two-hour break in the afternoon, and a final closing time of 10.30 or 11p.m. However, in Scotland regular extensions have broken down these restrictions in many areas, with some pubs opening all day (and night); see *Scottish Hours*.

Orange Clifton Inns home-brew pub, Pimlico, London. *Cask beers*: SW1 (1040), SW2 (1050).

Oranjeboom Dutch brewery in Rotterdam taken over by Britain's Allied Breweries in 1967. A weak 'Holland' lager (1033) is now brewed in Wrexham for bulk sale in Britain, under the 'orange tree' sign. Bottled Oranjeboom (1045) is imported.

Ordinary Popular name for standard bitters, notably from Youngs of London, where the Bitter (1036) is compared with the Special (1046).

Original Unoriginal name for usually stronger-than-average cask bitters from Whitbread Flowers (1044), Tolly Cobbold (1036), Greenall Whitley (1040). Also Wilson's cask mild (1032) and bitter (1036).

Original Brown Matthew Brown's bottled brown ale (1032) from Blackburn.

Original Gravity The British brewing industry's method of expressing the strength of beer. Pure water is defined as a gravity of 1000. Wort that is ready to start fermentation is denser than water, owing to the dissolved sugars; this density is measured by the Customs Officer to assess the Excise Duty. This is the Original Gravity. Most bitter beers have 'OGs' in the range 1035 to 1045, ie about 4% more dense than water. Fermentation converts the sugars into alcohol, reducing the density of the liquid; at the end of the fermentation period the beer reaches its *Final Gravity*. Final Gravities are normally in the region 1008–1015. The higher the figure, the sweeter the beer.

Original Light Dark keg beer (1032) from Alloa Brewery in Scotland.

Original Pale Vaux of Sunderland (1033) and Alloa of Scotland (1032) keg and canned light ale.

Orval An unusual skittle-shaped bottle marks out this distinctive triple-fermented Trappist beer (5.7 per cent alcohol) from the Abbaye of Orval in the far south of Belgium.

Owd Rodger Marston's notorious strong rich ale (1080), available both in cask and bottle.

Own Ale Miners Arms cask bitter (1040), Somerset.

Oyster Stout See *Castletown*.

[P]

PA Ridley's fine cask bitter (1034) from Essex. The initials are also used for a wide variety of light bitters or pale ales from the West Country, such as Whitbread's PA from Cheltenham.

Paine Brewery in St Neots, Cambridgeshire, formerly owned by Paines maltsters and millers, until sold off in 1982 and renamed James Paine. Owns 11 pubs, and in 1985 took over Robert Porter beer wholesalers in London. *Cask beers*: Mild (1032), XXX
(1036), St Neots Bitter (1041), EG (1047). *Keg*: As cask. *Bottled*: Pale Ale (1030), Brown Ale (1030), XXX (1036), EG (1047). Also for export: Cambridge Pale (1052), Special Red (1052), Royal Stag (1052), Kinross (1064).

Pale Ale A medium-gravity bottled ale, usually of about the same strength and hop rate as 'best bitter'. Some brewers produce a strong pale ale, of around 1045–1050 OG. One of the classic pale ales is Worthington White Shield, a naturally-conditioned beer. In the southwest, *PA*'s are low-gravity draught beers.

Pale Eighty Devanha's 80/- cask ale (1042) from Northeast Scotland.

Pale Malt General term for ale malts (excluding coloured malts such as chocolate malt).

Palmer Partly thatched family brewery in a delightful seaside setting in Bridport, Dorset, owning 70 pubs. *Cask beers*: BB (1030.4), IPA (1039.5), Tally Ho (1046). *Bottled*: Light Pale (1030), Nut Brown (1032), Extra Stout (1033), IPA (1038), Tally Ho (1046).

Parachute A contrivance somewhat like a funnel that sits in the fermenting vessel at the level of the yeast head; excess yeast spills over into the parachute and is drawn off.

Paradise Unusual new brewery set up in a Cornish bird park in Hayle in 1981, behind the one tied house, the Bird in Hand. *Cask beers*: Paradise Bitter (1040), Artists Ale (1055), Victory Ale (1070). Also bottled.

Paraflow The heat-exchanger that cools the wort from the near boiling-point at which it leaves the copper down to fermenting temperature (20–25°C).

Parish Wood's cask bitter (1040) from Shropshire.

Park Royal Guinness brewery in London supplying southern England. The northwest and Scotland are served from Dublin.

Parlour The landlord's own bar room, usually a seating area behind the bar front, sometimes in the landlord's private quarters. Admission is traditionally by invitation only. Such bars are now scarce.

Pasteurisation Heat treatment of filtered beer (bottled or keg) to kill off remaining yeast cells, leaving beer dead and sterile. Ensures that no further maturing can take place. Often gives the beer a 'cooked' flavour.

Paulaner The Munich brewery which created two German lager styles: the powerful Doppelbock (own brand Salvator) and the pale Münchner, which Paulaner today brews in both standard (Münchner Hell, 4.8 per cent alcohol) and original (Urtyp, 5.5 per cent) forms.

Pedigree The 'King of Bitters' from Marstons (1043), still brewed on the traditional Burton Union system at Burton-upon-Trent.

Peeterman The ungarnished version of the unique Belgian white beer, Hoegaards Wit, recreating the ancient beer style of Louvain.

Pelforth French brewery, based in Lille, famous for its top-fermenting beers, especially Pelforth Brune (1069), its strong brown ale. Also brews Killian's Irish Red Ale (1067) under licence (see *Killian*).

Pelham Ale Originally a bottled pale ale from Rayments of Furneux Pelham, Hertfordshire, now brewed by the parent company, Greene King (1031).

Pelican Pelican Export is the standard lager from the French Pelforth brewery.

Pendle Witches Brew Strong cask ale (1050) from Moorhouses of Burnley.

Pennine Webster's keg and tank bitter (1037) from Halifax.

Penn's Ale Premium cask bitter (1045) from Hoskins of Leicester.

Pensans Tiny Cornish brewery on a farm outside Penzance. *Cask beers*: MSB (1050), Coref Ertach Pensans (1055).

Pentland Drybrough's cask heavy (1036), named after the local Edinburgh hills.

Perrys Local keg beer produced by Irish Ale Breweries.

P.E.T. Polyethylene Terephthalate – a transparent, rigid plastic. P.E.T. bottles were introduced initially as large lemonade and cola containers but now are extensively used for beer, especially in supermarkets. Most common plastics are porous to carbon dioxide and so cannot be used for carbonated drinks. P.E.T. does not have this drawback and is therefore likely to make large inroads into the glass bottle and can markets.

Pewter An alloy of mostly tin with the addition of lead and sometimes copper and antimony. Formerly used for making the 'Pewter Pot' which was the standard pub drinking vessel until the 20th century. Nowadays, pewter mugs are mostly used for presentation purposes and as prizes for pub sports. Many locals have large collections of the regulars' private 'pewters', mostly illegal, being not government-stamped.

Pheasant & Firkin Bruce home-brew pub, London EC1. *Cask beers*: Pheasant Bitter (1036), Barbarian (1045), Dogbolter (1060).

Phillips Small Buckinghamshire brewery at the Greyhound pub, Marsh Gibbon, near Bicester. *Cask beers*: Heritage Bitter (1036), Ailric's Old Ale (1045). *Keg*: Hallerbrau Lager (1042).

Phoenix (1) Watney's south-coast company based in Brighton, with 470 pubs. No longer brews, but Tamplins Bitter (1038) is brewed for it in London. (2) Keg bitter from Irish Ale Breweries.

Phoenix & Firkin Bruce home-brew pub which rose out of the ashes of Denmark Hill railway station, London. *Cask beers*: Rail Ale (1036), Phoenix (1045), Dogbolter (1060).

Phoenix XXX Woodforde's strong bitter (1047), named after the way the brewery rose from the ashes after it was burnt down.

Pig & Whistle (1) Hampshire home-brew pub at Privett, supplying two Southampton pubs. *Cask beers*: Joshua Privett (1043), BDS (1055). (2) Glasgow home-brew pub in the Gorbals. *Cask beers*: Pig Light (1035), Pig Brew (1040).

Piggin A two-gallon cask. Rarely used today.

Pilgrim Surrey's first new brewery, set up in 1982 in Woldingham. *Cask beers*: Surrey Bitter (1038), Progress (1042), Talisman (1048).

Pils Short for Pilsener, but in Britain used to refer to a specific type of strong bottled lager. See *Diät Pils.*

Pilsener *or* **Pilsner** Golden hoppy lager originating in the Czech town of Pilsen in 1842, and now loosely copied around the world, often in a boring, bland style.

Pilsner Urquell The original – and best – Pilsener (5 per cent alcohol) from the Czech town of Plzen (Pilsen in German). Known in Bohemia as Plzensky Prazdroj, the beer is lagered in wooden casks for three months. Most British 'lagers' are lucky to get three weeks.

Pin A 4½-gallon cask. Now uncommon, owing to the expense of breweries handling such small quantities. See *Polypin*.

Pinkus Muller West German home-brew house in Münster, famous for its unusual pale version of Alt.

Pint Standard measure (⅛ gallon) in a pub, equal to 20 fluid ounces.

Piper Bass keg Scotch (1036) in the northeast, from Tennents. Also bottled Piper Export (1042).

Pitch After the malted grain is mashed and the liquid (wort) is run off into fermenting vessels, the fermentation is started by the addition of yeast. In brewery terms, this is the *pitching* of the yeast.

Pitfield Britain's first brewery in an off-licence, set up in the Beer Shop, London N1, in 1981. *Cask beers*: Bitter (1038), Hoxton Heavy (1048), Dark Star (1050) – also bottled.

Plain An Irish word for Porter. See also *Stout*.

Ploughman's Besides the ubiquitous pub lunch, Ploughman's Ale is Bateman's powerful XXXB in bottle (1049). An even stronger version (1060) is exported. Watneys also produce a weak Ploughman's Bitter (1032) in cans for the supermarket trade.

Plympton Hall's small real ale brewery at their Plympton depot, near Plymouth, producing Plympton Best (1039) and Plympton Pride (1045).

Poacher Whitbread's weak keg bitter (1032) for the south.

Pocket Brewers' term for the sack used for packaging hops.

Polish Term used by brewers to describe the fine filtering of a light-coloured beer to make it brilliant and crystal-clear before bottling or kegging.

Polypin A plastic bag, inside a rigid cardboard container, holding about 4½ gallons of beer. The mainstay of the take-home party trade.

Pommie's Revenge Strong cask ale (1060) from Goose Eye, Yorkshire – brewed in response to the invasion of imitation 'Australian' lagers.

Pompey Royal Whitbread's premium cask bitter (1043) for Wessex, brewed at Cheltenham.

Pony Beer glass size, usually ⅓ pint.

Pony Ales Beers from the Guernsey Brewery of St Peter Port. Name particularly given to the bottled mild (1037.7).

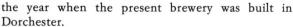

Poole Dorset's only new brewery, set up in 1981, which in 1983 added a home-brew pub in Poole called the Brewhouse. *Cask beer*: Dolphin Best (1038) – also bottled. See *Brewhouse*.

Pope's 1880 Eldridge Pope's keg and bottled beer (1041), named after the year when the present brewery was built in Dorchester.

Porter A dark, slightly sweetish but hoppy ale made with roasted barley; the successor of 'entire' and predecessor of stout. Porter originated in London around 1730, and by the end of the 18th century was probably the most popular beer in England. It was usually matured in vast vats, and in 1814, when a porter vat at Meux's London brewery in Tottenham Court Road burst, the resulting flood of nearly 130,000 gallons of ale drowned eight people. The fashion for the pale ales of Burton-upon-Trent ended the popularity of porter in the mid-19th century. In recent years, a number of brewers have revived porter, eg Timothy Taylor of Yorkshire and Woodfordes of Norfolk.

Pottsville Porter A dark 'roasted' beer (5 per cent alcohol) from the USA's oldest brewers, Yuengling of Pennsylvania. Such brews demonstrate the East Coast's British ale heritage.

Powell Central Wales beer wholesaler at Newtown, operating under the name Powell's Eagle Brewery, which took over the neighbouring Powys Brewery in 1983 to brew Samuel Powell Traditional Bitter (1040).

Premier Moorhouses of Burnley cask bitter (1036), which in 1983 became the first beer from a new brewery to win a medal at the major brewing exhibition, Brewex.

Premium Gibbs Mew's cask bitter (1039) from Salisbury. Also the name for any stronger-than-average beer – for which you pay a premium price, of course.

Primary Fermentation The main fermentation of the beer in the brewery fermentation vessels, applicable to all beers, traditional or processed.

Prime Certain beers have a small quantity of sugar solution added to each cask as it is filled. This *priming* with *priming sugar* encourages the secondary fermentation and adds some sweetness and colour. Excise regulations require a special licence for premises where priming is conducted.

Prince's Ale One of Britain's strongest beers (1100), from St Austell, Cornwall, originally bottled to celebrate Prince Charles's 21st birthday. Reputedly inflammable!

Private Reserve Drybrough's bottled strong ale (1056) from Edinburgh.

Prize Brew Truman's keg light mild (1032).

Prize Medal Charrington's bottled light ale (1035).

Prize Old Ale Britain's only naturally-conditioned beer sold in a corked bottle. Gales of Horndean, Hampshire, mature this powerful, rich ale (1095) for many months before bottling in conventional nip-size bottles or by hand in splendid half-pint corkers.

Progress Cask best bitter (1042) from Pilgrim Brewery, Surrey.

Prost Higsons of Liverpool weak canned lager (1031), named after the German for 'cheers'.

Pub A house open to the public at stated times for the purpose of social drinking – Britain's greatest social institution.

Public Bar The basic drinking bar of a pub, with the emphasis on games like darts and dominoes rather than soft furnishings. Increasingly threatened by pub 'improvements'.

Publican The keeper of a public house. Also called host, landlord, licensee, and so on.

Puncheon A 72-gallon cask, now only of historic

interest.

Pundy A Scottish term, dating from the 17th century, for second mash, low-gravity beer, also known as small beer. Term replaced by 'Table Beer' in the late 19th century; currently used to describe the free allowance of beer issued to brewery workers. See also *Strong Ale*.

[Q]

Quart Two pints. Until the early part of this century, a common size of serving mug.

Quarter Standard measure of barley (448lbs) as bought by the maltster. Each quarter should yield about 336lbs of malt and in turn yield 80–100lbs of extract for the brewer.

Queen Victoria Home-brew pub, London SE18. *Cask beers*: Country (1036), Sidekick (1047), Winter Ale (1054).

[R]

Rack When a cask or keg is filled with beer, the beer is *racked* into the cask. In the brewery this is done on the *racking line*. *Racked beer*, more specifically, however, is beer that has been transferred from a cask or tank in which it has been allowed to settle into a cask that may then be moved and used at once – for example, for an outside event.

Railway Whitbread home-brew pub (using malt extract) at Burgess Hill, Sussex. *Cask beers*: Burgess Best (1036), Railway Special (1048).

Rainier One of America's few ales of distinction, from Seattle, Washington, known as the Green Death because of its green label and high alcohol content (7.25 per cent).

Raker Wadworth's weak keg bitter (1030) from Wiltshire.

Ram Rod Young's Special in bottle (1046), named after the London brewery's mascot.

Ram Tam Timothy Taylor's fruity winter ale (1043) from Yorkshire.

Randall Guernsey's smaller Vauxlaurens Brewery in St Peter Port, operating under the VB Bobby Ales sign as distinct from Guernsey Brewery's Pony Ales. Real ale in a third of the 17 pubs. *Cask beers*: Best Mild (1036), Best Bitter (1046). *Keg*: Bitter (1046), Regal Lager (1045). *Bottled*:

Bobby Ale (1036), Stout (1043), IPA (1046). Not related to Randalls Vautier.

Randalls Vautier Jersey's oldest brewery, founded in 1832, unfortunately producing no real ale, though some of its 30 pubs stock Draught Bass. Chairman Edward Greenall also heads Grunhalle International on the island, which licenses Greenall Whitley and Devenish to brew this 'Bavarian' lager. *Keg beers*: Local Bitter (1036), Top Island (1042), Grunhalle (1038), Export Gold (1045). *Bottled*: Pale Ale (1035), Brown Ale (1035), Grunhalle (1038), DB Pils (1038).

Rauchbier The dark 'smoked' beers of Bamberg, Bavaria, are produced from malt fire-dried over beechwood logs. This gives the resulting 1055 brew a distinctive roasted flavour. The best-known brand is Kaiserdom but the most memorable is from the Schlenkerla home-brew house.

Raven First of the new wave of breweries in Sussex, which closed and then reappeared under new management in Brighton in 1983. Two tied houses. *Cask beers*: Bitter (1036), Best Bitter (1048), Old Master (1060).

Rayment Greene King's subsidiary Hertfordshire brewery at Furneux Pelham, with real ale in virtually all 24 pubs. *Cask beer*: BBA (1036). *Bottled*: Pelham Ale (1031) – now brewed at Bury St Edmunds.

Real Ale A name for draught (or bottled) beer brewed

from traditional ingredients, matured by secondary fermentation in the container from which it is dispensed, and served without the use of extraneous carbon dioxide; also called 'cask-conditioned' and 'naturally-conditioned' beer. Name coined by CAMRA, the Campaign for Real Ale.

Red Crown Bottled pale ale (1034) from Everards of Leicester.

Red Dragon (RD) Brain's dark cask mild (1035) from Cardiff. The Welsh red dragon is the brewery's symbol, shared with fellow South Wales brewers, Felinfoel of Llanelli.

Red Rose Greenall Whitley bottled stout (1040) from Warrington.

Red Seal Castletown's bottled pale ale (1036) from the Isle of Man.

Red Stripe The West Indies' best-known lager, from Jamaica, brewed under licence in Britain by Charles Wells of Bedford (1044).

Reekin' Scottish slang term for smelling of drink.

Reepham Small Norfolk brewery set up in 1983. *Cask beers*: Granary Bitter (1038), Brewhouse Ale (1055), Barley Wine (1078).

Regal Holt's backward lager (1039) from Manchester. Also Randall's keg lager from Guernsey (1045).

Reigate Tiny brewery (using malt extract) in John Landregan off-licence, Reigate, Surrey. *Cask beer*: Reigate Bitter (1042).

Reinheitsgebot German beer purity law, dating from 1516, which rigidly decrees that the only ingredients which may be used in the brewing of beer are water, barley or wheat, hops, and yeast. Chemical additives, widely used in the British brewing industry, are banned. Even sugar is not allowed.

Resch's KB Despite the name, this is an Australian lager produced by Tooths of Sydney.

Riding North Country Breweries of Hull cask bitter (1038), named after the old Yorkshire county divisions.

Ridley Essex's surviving family brewery

still producing fine, good-value 'beers from the wood' for its 65 pubs around Chelmsford. Won the first ever CAMRA beer award at the exhibition at Alexandra Palace in 1978, for their PA bitter. *Cask beers*: XXX (1034), PA (1034), HE (1045), Bishops (1080). *Bottled*: Brown Ale (1030), Essex Ale (1030), Old Bob (1050), Stock Ale (1050), Bishops Ale (1080). Also brew for Cooks.

Right Arm Slang term for drinking – 'exercise my right arm'. The lever used to raise the glass to the lips (except in left-handed drinkers!).

Ringwood Hampshire brewery set up by one of the fathers of the new brewery movement, Peter Austin, in 1978. Three tied houses. *Cask beers*: Best Bitter (1040), Fortyniner (1049), Old Thumper (1060) – also bottled.

Road House A large pub of the inter-war period catering for motor car and coach trade, particularly at the outer edges of large urban areas and along arterial roads. With the advent of the breathalyser, now being converted apace to steakhouses etc.

Roasted Barley Kilned un-malted barley, dark in colour, used mainly to add colour to stouts and porters.

Robin Hood Home of Nottingham's bottled pale ale (1045). An archer is the brewery symbol.

Robinson Stockport family brewery with over 300 pubs in the northwest and Wales, which in 1982 took over Hartleys of Cumbria. One of the few breweries still using wooden casks. *Cask beers*: Best Mild (1032), Bitter (1035), Best Bitter (1041), Old Tom (1080). *Keg*: Cock Robin (1035), Einhorn Lager (1035). *Bottled*: Brown Ale (1037), Pale Ale (1041), Old Tom (1080), Einhorn (1035).

Rochefort The third Belgian Trappist Abbaye brewery in the foothills of the Ardennes, producing a similar range of beers to Chimay.

Rolling Rock A cult American lager from the Latrobe Brewery, Pennsylvania, with most of its character in its name. Immortalised in the film *The Deer Hunter*.

Romford Allied's London brewery producing a range

of cask bitters for Ind Coope's southeast companies. Also runs its own 75 Romford Brewery pubs. *Cask beers*: Benskins Bitter (1037), Brewers Bitter (1037), Friary Meux (1037), Taylor Walker (1037). *Keg*: Benskins Pale (1032), John Bull (1036), Skol (1037). *Bottled*: John Bull (1036), High Life (1032), Skol (1035). *Canned only*: Falcon (1032).

Rope A bacterial infection of beer, much dreaded by the brewer. The infective agent is an anaerobic bacterium called Zymamonas, whose action produces slimy gelatinous threads in the beer – a cask can be completely ruined in a matter of hours. 'Ropey' beer has given the language the general slang expression for bad or poor quality.

Rose & Crown Tetley home-brew pub, York. *Cask beer*: Viking Bitter (1043).

Rose Street Scotland's first new home-brew pub, set up by Alloa Brewery in Edinburgh. *Cask beer*: Auld Reekie (1037).

Round The buying of drinks for everyone in one's company.

Rouse A brewer's way of saying 'stir' or 'mix'. For example, fermenting wort may be *roused* from time to time: traditionally with large wooden paddles but now more commonly by injection of air bubbles, or by recycling the wort – pumping it in a fan-shaped spray back across the yeast head.

Royal (1) Tolly Cobbold's bottled barley wine (1064) from Suffolk. **(2)** Scottish & Newcastle's lager brewery in Manchester, producing Harp, Kestrel etc, which in 1986 will also start to brew ales.

Royal Clarence Home-brew pub at Burnham-on-Sea, Somerset. *Cask beer*: KC Bitter (1038).

Royal Inn Home-brew pub at Horsebridge on the Devon–Cornwall border. *Cask beers*: Tamar (1039), Horsebridge Best (1045), Heller (1060).

Royal Oak Eldridge Pope's strong cask ale (1048) reintroduced in 1975 – similar to their draught beer of 1896, claim the Dorset brewers. Now also bottled.

Royal Sovereign Best bitter (1040) from Kentish Ales, Tunbridge Wells. Also Royal Pale (1035) and Porter (1050).

Royal Stag Bottled strong ale (1052) brewed for export by Paines of Cambridgeshire.

Rubidy *or* **Rubbity** *or* **Rubberdy** Australian term for a pub. Derives from rhyming slang *rub-a-dub-dub*.

Ruddles One of the most famous real ale brewers, from Rutland, Leicestershire, with a far from traditional trade. In 1977 the Langham family firm sold its 37 pubs to finance expansion of the brewery, to supply packaged beer to supermarkets and its celebrated County to the free trade. Over 400 Watney pubs in London now also take the strong draught ale. *Cask beers*: Rutland Bitter (1032), County (1050). *Keg*: As cask. *Bottled*: Rutland (1032), County (1050), Barley Wine (1080), plus a wide variety of own-label bottles for supermarkets.

Rupert Group This Rothmans cigarette and Intercontinental Breweries group of South Africa has international links with United Breweries (Carlsberg and Tuborg) of Denmark and Carling of Canada.

Russet Ale Elgood's bottled mild (1032) from Wisbech in the Fens.

Russian Stout Remarkable, powerful bottle-conditioned stout, reputedly made popular by Empress Catherine the Great, and originally produced by London brewers for export to the Baltic. Courage still produce an occasional batch of this 1100 beer which is matured for over a year in the brewery. The nip-size bottles are year-dated and will keep for many years.

Rutland Ruddles bitter (1032), named after the old county championed by the brewery.

[S]

SA Brain's best bitter (1042) from Cardiff, where this cask special ale is popularly known as 'Skull Attack'.

Saaz The internationally revered hops from the Czechoslovak region of Bohemia, centred on the town of Zatec.

Saccharometer An instrument used to measure the sugar content of the wort, usually in the form of a hydrometer. There is also the *saccharimeter*, which measures sugar concentrations by changes in optical properties.

Saccharomyces Scientific name for yeast. *S. cerevisiae* is the top-fermenting ale yeast; *S. uvarum* (formerly *S. carlsbergensis*) is the bottom-fermenting lager yeast.

Sack Brewers' term for the plastic or hessian container used for packaging malt.

St Austell Independent Cornish brewery in St Austell with 132 pubs in the county, most serving real ale. *Cask beers*: BB (1031), XXXX (1034), Tinners Ale (1038), Hicks Special (1050). *Keg*: BB (1031), Duchy – formerly Extra (1037). *Bottled*: Brown Ale (1032), Light Ale (1031), Duchy (1038), Smugglers (1070), Prince's Ale (1100).

St Christopher Allied's alcohol-free bottled lager.

St David's Porter Felinfoel's 'beefed up' brown ale (1036), chiefly exported in bottle from South Wales to America.

St Edmund Greene King's powerful bottled ale (1060) from East Anglia, originally brewed in 1970 to mark the 1100th anniversary of the martyrdom of St Edmund, from whom GK's home-town of Bury St Edmunds takes its name.

St James's Gate Guinness brewery in Dublin, claimed to be the largest brewery in Europe.

St Leonard The most widely available French Bière de Garde (laying-down beer), from Boulogne.

St Neots Cask and keg best bitter (1041) from Paines

of Cambridgeshire.

St Sixtus This Abbaye at Westvleteren produces the strongest beer in Belgium, Abt, with 12 per cent alcohol, besides two other Trappist beers. As the abbey brewery is small, the beers for public sale are brewed to the same recipe by the nearby commercial brewery, St Bernardus.

Sair Home-brew pub at Linthwaite, Huddersfield. *Cask beers*: Linfit Mild (1032), Bitter (1035), Special (1041), Old Eli (1050), Leadboiler (1063), Enoch's Hammer (1080).

Saladin Boxes Huge uncovered open-ended rectangular boxes used for modifying barley during the malting process.

Salisbury Gibbs Mew's cask best bitter (1042) from Wiltshire.

Saloon Essentially the same as *Lounge*, except in the USA where Southern Comfort and six-guns are the order of the day.

Salvator The very first German Doppelbock or 'double bock' beer, now produced by the Paulaner brewery of Munich.

Sam Brown Webster's (1034) and Mitchells & Butlers' (1035) bottled brown ales.

Samichlaus The world's strongest beer, brewed by Hurlimann of Switzerland, containing 14 per cent alcohol. 'Santa Claus' does not start with the highest original gravity (1102), but is lagered for a whole year to produce its mighty strength.

Sampson Truman's strong cask ale (1055), named after one of the London brewery's original partners, Sampson Hanbury.

Samson Vaux's challenger to Cameron's Strongarm in the manly northeast (1042). Also the name of a local rival to the famous Budvar (Budweiser) brewery in Czechoslovakia, producing a dark lager called Dalila!

Samuel Whitbread Whitbread's premium cask and keg bitter (1044), named after the brewing giant's founder.

S&P Norwich cask bitter (1038), named after one of the local breweries, Steward & Patteson, absorbed by

Watneys.

Sanwald Stuttgart brewers specialising in German Weizen (wheat) beers.

Sarum Special Gibbs Mew's strong bottled pale ale (1048) from Salisbury.

SAS Strong Anglian Special (1048) cask beer from Crouch Vale, Essex. Motto: 'He who dares!'.

Satzenbrau Harp's Germanic-sounding bottled Pils (1047) brewed in the well-known German cities of London and Dundalk, Eire.

Saxon Devenish keg bitter (1033) for Cornwall.

Saxon Cross Trade name of Winkle's brewery and beers, Buxton, Derbyshire.

SBA Donnington's special bitter ale (1042) from the Cotswolds.

SBB Crown Brewery's cask Special Bitter Beer (1036) from South Wales.

Schaapskooi The only Dutch Trappist brewery, producing the bottle-conditioned ale, La Trappe, from the abbey near Tilburg.

Schlenkerla A German home-brew tavern in Bamberg, Bavaria, dating back to 1678, and producing the most intense of the town's famous Rauchbiere (smoked beers).

Schlitz The beer that made Milwaukee famous was once the largest brewing company in America. Then the quality of its product slipped and so did its standing. Today the Milwaukee brewery is closed and the company taken over by rivals Stroh, though the bland beer (1045) is now available in Britain.

Schultheiss Berlin's major brewery, known for its Weisse (white) beer. With Dortmunder Union, it forms one of the largest brewing groups in West Germany.

Scotch Ale The term 'Scotch Ale' is more in use in the northeast of England than in Scotland. Most beers sold as 'Scotch' are the same as 'heavy', the Scottish 70/- ale, eg Lorimer's Best Scotch from Edinburgh, sold by Vaux. In Belgium this means a strong dark bottled beer like Gordons from Scottish & Newcastle, brands which are not available in Britain. There are also stronger 'Christmas Ales' under the same names.

Scottish Ale The name of Belhaven's bottled export (1041) when actually exported to America.

Scottish & Newcastle The smallest of the Big Six brewers in Britain, with less than 1,500 pubs, the vast majority in Scotland and the northeast. Owes its national standing to the penetration of its McEwan and Younger beers in the free trade. Operates four breweries: Fountain and Holyrood in Edinburgh, Tyne in Newcastle, and Royal in Manchester. Holyrood is due to close in 1986. In 1984 tried to expand by taking over Camerons of Hartlepool, but failed after opposition from CAMRA when the deal was referred to the Monopolies Commission. Also owns 43 Thistle Hotels and Waverley Vintners. See *Scottish Brewers* and *Newcastle Breweries*.

Scottish Brewers Scottish arm of Scottish & Newcastle, with 558 pubs, formed in 1931 through the merger of Edinburgh brewers, William Younger and McEwan. A new brewery was built on McEwan's Fountainbridge site in 1974, and the old Younger brewery at Holyrood is due to close in 1986. *Cask beers*: McEwan 70/- or Younger's Scotch (1036.5), McEwan 80/- or Younger's IPA (1042), Younger's No 3 (1043). *Keg*: Like cask, the same beer is sold under both McEwan and Younger names, often under a bewildering variety of regional terms: Light Mild or Pale (1032), Dark Mild or Light (1032), Scotch or Heavy (1036), Tartan Bitter or Special (1036), McEwan's Export or Special (1042), Harp (1032), Kestrel (1032), McEwan's Lager (1038). *Bottled*: Light or Pale Ale (1032), Brown Ale (1032), Blue Label (1032), Sweet Stout (1032), McEwan's Export (1042), Double Century (1054), McEwan's Strong (1068), Harp (1032). *Canned only*: Monk Export (1042).

Scottish Hours Standard Scottish pub opening hours are: Monday to Saturday, 11a.m.–2.30p.m. and 5–11p.m; Sundays 12.30–2.30p.m. and 6.30–11p.m. However, 'regular extension' licences may allow pubs to remain open during the afternoon and indeed prior to 11a.m. and after 11p.m. The actual hours vary a great deal within each region according to the whims of the licensing boards. This new licensing arrangement is often referred to as the 'Scottish Experiment'.

Scottish Pride Drybrough's weak canned lager (1032), Edinburgh.

Sealord Southsea's strong ale (1060) from Portsmouth.

Secondary Fermentation After the *primary fermentation*, beers that are to be cask-conditioned are racked into the casks together with some residual yeast. This yeast continues a slow secondary fermentation in the cask – all-important if the beer's full flavour is to develop. True lagers also have a secondary fermentation but in large refrigerated tanks known as lagering tanks.

Sediment The sludgy material that settles out of cask-conditioned beer by the action of the finings. It consists mostly of dead yeast cells but also contains some proteins, and some hops if the cask was dry hopped.

Selby Old Yorkshire family brewery that began brewing again in 1972 after a gap of 18 years. One tied house. *Cask beer*: Best Bitter (1039), bottled as No 1.

Sensible Modicum Immortalised phrase following the trial for drunk-driving of a Scottish judge, who said in his defence that he had consumed only a 'sensible modicum' of whisky.

Set Mash An occasional problem with a mash where the whole mixture becomes very sticky and the wort will not drain off properly.

Sevenoaks Small Kent brewery at the Crown Point Inn, Seal Chart, since 1981, supplying local free trade. *Cask beers*: Best Bitter (1038), Crown Point BB (1038).

70/- Ale Scottish term for medium-gravity beers. Usually 1034–1039 and light in colour. Term synonymous with 'Heavy' in Scotland. See *Shilling System*.

Severn Bore Best bitter (1045), Jolly Roger Brewery, Upton-on-Severn, Worcs.

Shandy A half-and-half mixture of beer and lemonade. Bottled shandy is virtually non-alcoholic.

Sheaf The barley sheaf is a popular symbol for British breweries, like Wards of Sheffield. But Sheaf Stout is surprisingly produced by Australian brewers, Tooths.

Sheffield Best Bitter Ward's cask and keg bitter (1038) from Sheffield.

Sheffield Stout Not a stout at all, but a mixture of Black Beer and lemonade. See *Black Beer*.

Shefford Cask bitter (1038) from Banks & Taylor, Shefford, Beds.

Shepherd Neame The hop county of Kent's only surviving independent, brewing a typically hoppy range of beers at Faversham for their 250 pubs. *Cask beers*: Master Brew Mild (1031), Master Brew Bitter (1036), Stock Ale (1036), Invicta Best Bitter (1044), Five X (1044). *Keg*: Master Brew XX (1033), Abbey (1039), Hurlimann Sternbrau (1045). *Bottled*: Light Ale (1033), Borough Brown (1034), Abbey Ale (1045), Bishop's Finger (1053), Christmas Ale (1068), Sternbrau (1045).

Shilling System A code of beer grading used in Scotland. The system of marking beers 70/-, 80/-, etc, was first used in the 1870s as the gross invoice price for a barrel of beer (net price was always different as it included discounts and sundry costs), i.e. an 80/- ale would never actually cost the publican £4. Because of the progressive beer duty levied in Britain, where higher gravity beers are taxed more, the higher the shilling mark, the stronger the beer. An 80/- beer would always be stronger than a 60/- beer.

Shipstone Nottingham brewery taken over by regional giant Greenall Whitley of Warrington. Real ale in virtually all 270 pubs, but the bitter is no longer so distinctive. *Cask beers*: Mild (1034), Local Bitter (1037). *Keg*: Same as cask. *Bottled*: Nut Brown (1034), Gold Star (1034), Ship Stout (1042). See also *Greenall Whitley*.

Ship Stout Shipstone of Nottingham bottled stout (1042).

Shive A wooden bung, several inches in diameter, used to stop up the bung hole through which the cask is filled. A small

117

central piece of the shive (the *tut*) is knocked through to vent the cask via the spile hole.

Shout Slang term for a round of drinks.

Shrewsbury & Wem See *Wem*.

Siegel The Pils brand from the German giant, Dortmunder Union.

Silver Special Charles Wells keg light mild (1030) from Bedford.

Silverthorne Small South Wales brewery, originally known as Gwent Ales when set up in 1981. Now sited in Cwmbran. Has one pub. *Cask beers*: Best Bitter (1035), Special (1040), Exhibition (1054), Druid's Ale (1072), Celtic Gold (1046). *Keg*: Springvale Bitter (1033).

Simonds Courage's light keg bitter (1032) in the south, named after the former Reading brewery taken over by Courage, Barclay in 1960.

Simpkiss Black Country family brewers in Brierley Hill with a much-improved range of real ales for their 16 pubs. *Cask beers*: AK (1036), Bitter (1037), Supreme (1043), Old (1050), TNT (1050). *Keg*: Bitter (1037). *Bottled*: Extra Special (1038), Black Country Old (1052).

Sixex Holt's bottled barley wine (1064) from Manchester.

Six-pack Popular term for a take-home pack of bottled or canned beer, commonly used in the USA.

Six-rowed Barley Barleycorns that grow in six-rowed ears, more common outside the UK, especially in the USA. Compare *Two-rowed Barley*.

Sixty Alice Brewery strong ale (1060) from Inverness.

60/- Ale Scottish term for mild beers. Usually 1030–1034 and dark in colour. Synonymous with 'Light' in Scotland. See *Shilling System*.

6X Wadworth's most famous cask bitter (1040) from Wiltshire, which even provoked a drinkers' campaign in the late 1970s when a Ministry of Agriculture proposal to grade beer strengths in Xs again would have banned its name. The Ministry lost that argument 6X–nil.

Skim To remove periodically the excess yeast from the top of the fermenting vessel. Much of this surplus yeast goes to make yeast extracts such as 'Marmite'.

Skinful Slang term for a large consumption of beer.

Skol One of the world's mass-produced international lagers, brewed from Bulgaria to the West Indies. First produced in Holland in 1959, Skol International is almost wholly owned by Allied Breweries who manufacture keg Skol (1037) in Britain in Romford, Burton, Wrexham, and Alloa. Bottled and canned version (1035) is weaker. Also Skol Special Strength (1046).

Skona Hall & Woodhouse's weak lager (1032) from Dorset, only available in cans, chiefly for grocery stores.

Skull Attack This popular name for Brain's cask SA best bitter (1042) from Cardiff serves warning of what can happen after sliding down a few.

Slalom Matthew Brown's lager (1036) from the ski slopes of the Lakeland Lager Brewery in Workington. There's also a stronger keg and bottled Slalom D (1045) and a super-strength Slalom International (1068).

Slate Square See *Square*.

Sleeve A straight glass with no handle.

Small Beer See *Pundy* and *Strong Ale*.

Smiles Happy name for Avon's first new brewery, set up in Bristol in 1977. *Cask beers*: Best Bitter (1040), Exhibition (1051).

Smith, John John Smith is the northern arm of Courage, taken over in 1970, and arch Tadcaster rival of the independent and once related Samuel Smith (see below). The magnificent Victorian brewery, built in 1884, did not brew any real ale at all for ten years, until cask John Smith's Bitter was reintroduced in 1984. *Cask beer*: Bitter (1036). *Keg*: Tawny Light (1032), Chestnut (1033), Midlands Mild (1036), Bitter (1036), Old Tom (1037), Magnet (1040), J. Smith's Lager (1036). *Bottled*: Sweet Stout (1039), Double Brown (1041), Magnet Pale (1042), Export (1055), Magnet Old (1070).

Smith, Samuel Samuel Smith is Yorkshire's oldest brewery, dating back to 1758, which unlike its Tadcaster neighbours, John Smith, is still independent and highly traditional, using slate squares and wooden casks. Has recently extended its range of real ales for its

300 pubs including 16 in London. Also produces a wide range of distinctive bottled beers. *Cask beers*: Old Brewery Bitter (1038.9), Tadcaster Bitter (1035), XXXX (1033). *Keg*: Mild (1032), XXXX (1033), Tadcaster Bitter (1035), Sovereign (1037), OBB (1038.9), Ayingerbrau (1039), D Pils (1047). *Bottled*: Light (1033), Nut Brown (1034), Pale Ale (1037), OBB (1040), Sweet Stout (1042), Nourishing Stout (1050), Strong Pale (1045), Strong Brown (1045), Strong Golden (1100), Ayingerbrau (1039), D Pils (1047), Special (1081). Also for export: Pale Ale (1050), Famous Taddy Porter (1050), Celebrated Oatmeal Stout (1050), Nut Brown (1050).

Smithwicks Eire's main keg and bottled ale (1036), from Kilkenny. Part of the Guinness-controlled Irish Ale Breweries.

Smoked Beer See *Rauchbier*.

Smoke Room The forerunner of the Lounge, especially in the north of England. Originally a room where customers retired to smoke.

Smugglers St Austell's dark bottled barley wine (1070) from Cornwall.

Snob Screen A pivoted decorated screen above the bar counter, designed (in Victorian pubs) to allow 'snobs' to drink in private, without being observed by their social inferiors across the bar. In these more egalitarian times, snob screens remain prized features of a few pubs.

Snug A small room in a pub for private drinking; nowadays usually knocked through into larger bars.

Somerset Special Hardington's premium cask bitter (1043) from Somerset.

SOS Shefford Old Strong (1050) from Banks & Taylor, Bedfordshire.

Southdown Gales keg bitter (1040) from Hampshire.

Southsea Small Portsmouth brewery set up in the Old Lion Brewery buildings in 1982, now with one pub, the Brewery Tap, nearby. *Cask beers*: Bosun Dark (1032), Captain's Bitter (1037), Admiral's Ale (1048), Sealord (1060).

Sovereign Sam Smith's keg bitter (1037) from Tadcaster.

SPA Wethered's Special Pale Ale (1041) from Marlow, Bucks.

Sparge Towards the end of the mash, as the wort is drawn off, the mash is sparged by spraying some more hot liquor onto the top of the grains to flush out the last fermentables. Usually the spray is from rotating, perforated tubes called sparge arms.

Sparkler A device attached to the beer engine outlet. The beer is forced through very small orifices to aerate it and produce a creamy 'tight head'. The amount of aeration can be varied, so ask for the sparkler to be screwed up for a creamy head or screwed out for a 'flat' pint.

Sparkling Ale A term historically used by brewers to indicate that their bottled beer is filtered. Ironically, the chief beer still carrying this title, Cooper's Sparkling Ale from Australia, contains sediment.

Spaten A pioneer lager brewery, Spaten of Munich developed both the dark Münchner beer and the stronger Marzenbier. Its Münchner Dunkel Export (5 per cent alcohol) and Ur-Marzen (5.8) are classics of their styles.

Special Much over-used word to describe very ordinary beers such as Watney's Special. Occasionally justified, as in Young's Special (1046).

Special Red Paine's strong bottled ale (1052) for export.

Spent Grains Brewers' term for left-over malt grains after mashing. Usually sold for cattle fodder.

Spile A small wooden peg inserted into the vent hole at the top of the cask (in the shive). A soft spile is porous and allows excess carbon dioxide to escape slowly; a hard spile is used to seal the cask completely after venting or when not in service (to prevent entry of air or loss of too much gas).

Spingo Collective name of the beers brewed at the Blue Anchor, Helston, Cornwall.

Spoiled Beer To the brewer this has a precise meaning – beer that is in some way spoiled while it is still at the brewery and on which the excise duty will be reclaimed.

Sport Keg lager (1036) from the Leicester Brewery.

Spread Eagle See *Woodforde*.

Springfield Bass, Mitchells & Butlers Wolverhampton brewery. *Cask and keg*: Springfield Bitter (1036). Also brews for Charrington.

Springvale Silverthorne's keg bitter (1033) from South Wales.

Square A particular traditional form of fermenting vessel of a square shape, formerly made of stone or slate slabs although new ones are stainless steel. The top is partially covered in, with a central hole to allow the escape of yeast and carbon dioxide. Especially common in the north, they are often known as Yorkshire Squares.

Squires Blackawton premium cask beer (1044) from Devon.

Stag Watney's premium cask beer (1044), named after the Stag Brewery, Mortlake. Also canned.

Stallion Small brewery next to the Long Barn pub, Chippenham, Berks. *Cask beers*: Stallion Bitter (1037), Barnstormer (1048).

Standard Buckley's basic cask and keg bitter (1032) from Llanelli, South Wales.

Starbright IPA Hardys & Hansons bottled pale ale (1039) from Nottingham.

Starlight Watney's low-gravity keg (1033).

Station Tetley home-brew pub (using malt extract) at Guiseley, Leeds. *Cask beer*: Guiseley Gyle (1045).

Steak House A large pub given over mostly to the sale of a small variety of standard meals. Berni, Cavalier, Beefeater are some of the chains.

Steam Beer A rare Californian method of brewing, using bottom-fermenting lager yeasts at ale temperatures. See *Anchor Steam*.

Steaming Scottish slang term for being drunk.

Steel's Masher A rotary mixing device which ensures a correct balance of grist and liquor at the predetermined strike heat, and runs the mixture into the mash tun. Patented in 1853.

Steep The water-absorption stage of the malting process, where the barley is allowed to soak in water prior to germination.

Stein Thwaites keg lager (1036) from Blackburn, named after a German drinking vessel. By agreement, Guernsey Brewery use the same name for their stronger lager (1048). Previously their lager was called Hi-Brau!

Steingold McMullen's premium lager (1042) from Hertford.

Stella Artois Belgium's biggest brewery, whose premium lager (1047) is brewed in Britain by Whitbread.

Sternbrau Shepherd Neame of Kent brew this beer under licence from Hurlimann of Switzerland – with more strength (1045) and character than most British lagers.

Stillage A wooden framework on which the casks are set up in the cellar. Also known as *Thralls* or *Horsing*.

Stingo A semi-sweet, lightly-hopped, potent barley wine of Yorkshire origin, formerly served when stale and flat after long maturation. Watney's still produce a dark bottled barley wine (1076) under this name, as do Higsons (1078) and Hall & Woodhouse (1066).

Stock Ale Traditionally a high-gravity beer matured for long periods (up to a year) in vat or cask. Few today are commercially available in Britain, though some breweries (eg Greene King) produce one for blending in the brewery. Godson of London brew a bottled and, in winter, cask Stock Ale, the gravity of which rises with the year (1085 in 1985). Shepherd Neame brew a much lower gravity draught Stock (1036), and Ridleys have a bottled Stock Ale (1050).

Stocks Small brewery based at the Hall Cross pub, Doncaster. *Cask beers*: Best (1037), Select (1044), Old Horizontal (1054).

Stones Bass Sheffield brewery producing a near-national cask and keg bitter (1038).

Stone Square See *Square*.

Stout One of the classic types of ale, a successor in fashion to 'porter'. Usually a very dark, heavy, well-hopped bitter ale, with a dry palate, thick creamy head, and good grainy taste contributed by a proportion of dark roasted barley in the mash. Guinness is the best-known bitter 'extra stout', of 1042 OG. The earliest uses of the word 'stout' indicate that it was applied to beers which were 'stout' in terms of strength; later, the word came to be associated with the idea of 'stout' in body, and was hence applied to the dark, full-bodied beer which was stronger and hoppier than porter. Ordinary stout in Ireland was comparable to 'plain porter'. See also *Sweet Stout*, *Russian Stout*.

Strathalbyn Small Scottish brewery set up in 1982 to challenge the keg stronghold of Glasgow. *Cask beers*: Strathalbyn I (1038), Strathalbyn II (1043).

Strong Ale Originally the partner of 'small beer'. The first wort run off the mash would produce what in Tudor times was referred to as 'doble' (=double strength), a strong ale for men. The mash tun would be refilled with hot liquor, and the weaker second run-off of wort would be used to produce 'syngl' (=single strength) or 'small beer' for women, children, and servants. Currently, any ale of over 1055 OG is generally regarded as a 'strong ale'.

Strongarm The major real ale in the northeast, brewed by Camerons of Hartlepool, though the strength of this premium bitter with the steelworker image has been reduced to a less muscle-bound 1040 gravity on draught. Bottled Strongarm Special is 1046.

Strong Country Whitbread's cask bitter (1037) for Wessex, named not after its potency but after Strong's brewery at Romsey which Whitbread closed in 1981. Brewed at Cheltenham.

Strong Golden Sam Smith's very powerful bottled barley wine (1100) from Yorkshire. Sams also produce Strong Brown and Strong Pale Ales (1045).

Strong Suffolk Greene King's bottled dark old ale (1056) from East Anglia, unusually blended from a powerful stock ale, matured in sealed oak vats for a year, and a fresher brew.

Stubby Australian term for a small beer bottle.

Sugar Brewers' sugar is an unrefined brown sugar, usually in block form. In many brews it is added to the wort at the copper boiling stage, increasing the fermentable material without requiring extra malt. In the past, landlords often added sugar to their casks in the pub cellar to re-ferment the beers to higher gravities (presumably increasing customer satisfaction). This illegal practice was so widespread that the licensing law carries a specific clause making it an offence for sugar to be found in a pub cellar.

Summerskill Devon brewery set up in a vineyard near Kingsbridge in 1983, which in 1985 moved to Plymouth. *Cask bitter*: Bigbury Best (1044).

Sunderland Draught bitter in cask and keg (1040) from Vaux of Sunderland.

Supalita Litre bottles of Gibbs Mew's pale ale (1031).

Super (1) Tennent's powerful bottled lager (1081) from Scotland. The strongest lager brewed in Britain. **(2)** Burtonwood's bottled brown ale (1032) from Cheshire.

Super Brew Bailey's premium cask beer (1047) from Worcestershire.

Super Mild Gibbs Mew's keg dark mild (1031) from Salisbury.

Supreme Premium cask bitters from Simpkiss of the Black Country and the new Abbey Brewery in Nottinghamshire. Both 1043.

Surrey Cask bitter (1038) from Pilgrim Brewery, Surrey.

Sussex Cask bitter and mild (1034) from the Horsham brewers, King & Barnes. Also used by Lewes brewers, Harvey, for their bitters, keg beer, and stout.

Swan Western Australia's major brewery, based in Perth, which obviously likes the birds. Besides Swan, it also produces Emu lager.

Sweetheart Tennent's bottled sweet stout (1035) from Scotland.

Sweet Stout Formerly called 'milk stout', until the Trade Descriptions Act ruled out the use of this terminology because the product does not contain milk. The 'milk' is a simple way of indicating that the stout's sweetness is derived from lactose. Mackeson is the best-known example.

Sweet Wort The liquid that is run off from the mash tun into the copper. Sweet wort contains all of the fermentable sugars that have been extracted from the malt.

Swifty Slang term for a quick drink, also known as a *swift one*.

[T]

Table Beer Another term for *Dinner Ale*.

Tadcaster Cask and keg bitter (1035) from Sam Smith of Yorkshire.

Taddy Ales Beers from Sam Smith of Tadcaster, Yorkshire.

Talisman Winter ale (1048) from Pilgrim Brewery, Surrey.

Tall Fount A tall pillar tap mounting stationed on a bar, used to dispense the majority of traditional beers in Scotland. Beer is driven to the fount by air pressure or by electric pump. Term derives from 'Fountain', but is pronounced 'Font'. Founts were first used in Scotland in the 1830s. Common names include: Aitken, Grosvenor, McGlashan, Mackie & Carnegie.

Tally Ho Hunting-call name for Palmer's strong summer cask ale (1046) from Dorset, and Adnams powerful bottled barley wine (1075) from Suffolk.

Tamplins Watney's Phoenix company's cask beer (1038), brewed in London. Named after the Brighton brewery Watneys took over in 1953.

Tanglefoot Hall & Woodhouse's aptly-named strong cask ale (1048) from Dorset.

Tankard Whitbread's fading keg best bitter (1037).

Tank Beer Brewery-conditioned bright beer that is delivered in bulk by road tanker and then pumped into large tanks in the cellar of the pub or club. These tanks are commonly of 90 or 180 gallon capacities. Tank beer is most common in the North of England, especially in the large social clubs.

Tannin One of the chemicals extracted from the hops during the boiling in the copper; has both preservative and bittering properties.

Tap The beer from a traditional cask is drawn off through an on-off tap that is driven into the cask. 'Tapping' is now often used as an expression for connection to any form of beer container, as in: 'This beer has only just been tapped' or 'I'll have to tap a new barrel'. Also part of a pub name, usually indicating a small basic pub that was an 'annexe' to a larger establishment.

Tap Room Basic public bar, traditionally where customers would sit alongside the stillaged casks of beer. The back bar of the Coopers Arms in Burton-upon-Trent is one of the more famous surviving examples.

Target A new disease-resistant variety of English hop, high in alpha acids.

Tartan Younger's ubiquitous keg and canned bitter (1036), known as 'Special' in Scotland.

Tavern A hostelry historically catering for local custom, as opposed to *Inn*. Also once the name for Courage's little-mourned keg beer.

Tawny Cask bitter (1040) from Cotleigh Brewery, Somerset. Also keg light mild (1032) from John Smith, Tadcaster.

Taylor Timothy Taylor's beers from Keighley, Yorkshire, are the quality ales of Britain, having won more championship medals than any other brewery. Their fame extends far beyond their 28 pubs. *Cask beers*: Golden Best or Bitter Ale (1033), Mild (1033), Best Bitter (1037), Landlord (1042), Porter (1043), Ram Tam (1043). *Bottled*: Special Pale (1033), Northerner (1033), Landlord (1042), Blue Label (1043), Black Bess Stout (1043).

Taylor Walker Ind Coope's London company with 600 pubs. Taken over in 1960, with the name revived in 1980. Beers are brewed at Romford and Burton. *Cask beer*: Bitter (1037). *Bottled*: Light Ale (1031.5).

Teetotaller A total abstainer from alcohol.

Tenant A licensee of a brewery-owned pub, held under a tenancy, as distinct from a salaried manager.

Tennent Caledonian Bass's Scottish company with breweries in Edinburgh and Glasgow. Best known for its lager, which has been brewed since 1885. *Cask beer*:

Heriot Brewery 80/-. *Keg*: Tennent's Light (1032), Bass Special (1035), Tennent's Special (1036), Piper Scotch (1036), Tennent's Export (1042), Tennent's Pilsner (1035), Tennent's Lager (1038), Tennent's Extra (1044). *Bottled*: As keg, apart from Sweetheart Stout (1035), Piper Export (1042) and Tennent's Super (1081). *Canned only*: Charger (1032).

1066 Goacher's draught winter brew (1066) from Kent. Also Alexandra's powerful keg beer (1064) from Brighton, after the date of the famous battle.

Tetley Leeds brewery which merged with Ind Coope and Ansells in 1961 to form Allied Breweries. Runs 1,100 pubs, mainly in Yorkshire, under the familiar Huntsman sign, 85 per cent of which serve real ale. Famous for the tight creamy head on its beers. *Cask beers*: Mild (1032), Falstaff (1032), Bitter (1035.5). *Keg*: As cask, plus Imperial (1042). *Bottled*: Special Pale (1037).

Tetley Walker Joshua Tetley's other half, west of the Pennines, with a brewery in Warrington, and real ale in 40 per cent of its 900 pubs. Merged with Tetley in 1960, just before Allied Breweries was formed. *Cask beers*: Tetley Mild (1032), Tetley Bitter (1035.5). *Keg*: As cask. *Bottled*: Brown Ale (1034), Bitter (1035.5). Also brews for its Liverpool subsidiary Peter Walker, and Holts of the Black Country. See *Walker*.

Texas Ale Belhaven's bottled ale (1056) from Scotland, specially brewed for export to the State of Texas.

Theakston Famous Yorkshire Dales family brewers at Masham since 1827, who bought the former State brewery in Carlisle in 1974 to meet demand for their real ales. Renowned for their Old Peculier. Taken over by Matthew Brown of Blackburn in 1984. *Cask beers*: Light Mild (1032.5), Best Bitter (1038), XB (1045), Old Peculier (1058.5). *Keg*: Dark Mild (1032.5), Black Bull (1035), Border Scotch (1035), plus same range as cask beers. *Bottled*: Pale Ale (1035), Special Brown (1047), plus Best Bitter, XB, and OP.

Thins Maltsters' term for rootlets and other waste shed

by barley during the malting process.

Thomas Hardy's Ale One of Britain's very few bottle-conditioned beers, and the strongest ale (1125) brewed in Britain. Eldridge Pope of Dorset first produced it in 1968 to mark the Wessex author's centenary. Each bottle, from a limited brewing each year, is individually numbered and dated. Will mature for 25 years – and should not be drunk before three! The alcohol content is over 12 per cent.

Thompson Devon brewery behind the London Inn, Ashburton, since 1981, supplying own pub and local free trade. *Cask beers*: Mild (1034), Bitter (1040), IPA (1045). *Keg*: Dartmoor Bitter (1037), Lager (1036). *Bottled*: Pale Ale (1045), IPA (1050) – both naturally-conditioned. Not to be confused with John Thompson.

Thorne Cask and keg bitter (1038) from Darley of Thorne, South Yorkshire.

Thralls See *Stillage*.

Three Counties Small Gloucester brewery set up in 1984, covering the three counties of Hereford, Worcester, and Gloucester, by the same brothers who run the Jolly Roger brewery. *Cask beer*: Three Counties Bitter (1040).

Three Crowns Phoenix home-brew pub, Ashurstwood, Sussex. *Cask beers*: Session Bitter (1038), Strong (1050).

Three Tuns Historic home-brew pub at Bishop's Castle, Shropshire. The old brewery actually dwarfs the pub. *Cask beers*: Mild (1035), XXX (1042), Castle Steamer (1045).

Thwaites Traditional Blackburn brewers with real ale in nearly all 390 pubs including one in London, which dented its popular image by taking over and closing down Yates & Jackson's Lancaster brewery in 1985. *Cask beers*: Mild (1032), Best Mild (1034), Bitter (1036). *Keg*: As cask, plus Stein Lager (1036). *Bottled*: Danny Brown (1034), East Lancs (1036), Big Ben (1050), Old Dan (1075).

Tie The means by which a brewery insists that a licensee sells their beers. Such a pub is called a tied house, as distinct from a free house.

Tiger Everards premium bitter (1041) , still produced at their Burton brewery which is now a working museum run by an independent trust. Also the name of a famous lager from Singapore brewed by Malayan Breweries, and the ale (1038) from the tiny Leyland 'shop' brewery, Lancs.

Tight Head See *Head*.

Timmermans One of Belgium's leading brewers of wild Lambic beers, from Itterbeek. Their bottled Gueuze is available in both 'naturelle' and filtered form.

Timothy Taylor See *Taylor*.

Tinners St Austell cask bitter (1038), named after the Cornish tin industry.

Tisbury Wiltshire brewery which has packed an eventful history of mergers and takeovers into its few years since it was launched in 1980 – with a share issue on the Stock Market. Now owned by a Sussex leisure company. *Cask beers*: Local Bitter (1037), Special (1045), Old Grumble (1060). *Keg and bottle*: Local and Old Grumble.

TNT Dynamite draught ale (1050) from Simpkiss of the Black Country.

Toby Charrington's Toby Jug trademark – now usually inside a red triangle since becoming Bass Charrington in 1967 – which lends its name to a wide variety of Bass beers. *Keg*: Toby Light (1032), Bitter (1033). *Bottled*: Light (1032), Brown (1032), Pale Ale (1044).

Tolly Cobbold Ipswich brewery with real ale in most of its 350 pubs. Linked with Camerons of Hartlepool as both were owned by Ellerman Lines, the shipping firm facing an uncertain future following a takeover by a hotel group. *Cask beers*: Mild (1032), Bitter (1034), Original (1036), Old Strong (1046). *Keg*: Bitter (1034), Best Bitter (1036). *Bottled*: Light (1032), Dark (1032), Export (1036), 250 (1073),

Royal (1064). Hansa keg lager (1036) is brewed by Camerons; DAB (1046) imported from Germany.

Tooley Street Small London brewery set up in 1984 primarily to serve the Dickens Inn, St Katherine's Dock, on the opposite bank of the Thames. *Cask beers*: Dickens Own or TSB (1040), Archway (1042), Special (1050).

Tooths The Australian rival to Castlemaine-Tooheys in Sydney, best known for its Resch's KB lager. Taken over by a shipping company in 1981.

Top Brass Wilson's bottled and canned lager (1033) from Manchester.

Top Brew Davenport's original award-winning dark strong ale (1071) in bottle. The Birmingham brewers then introduced a stronger golden version (1075), Top Brew De Luxe, which went on to win even more international medals. Advertised as 'strong as almost 2½ whiskies'.

Top Fermentation Fermentation in which the yeast rises to the top of the vessel in a thick foamy head. This is the method used for producing British ales, requiring a yeast of the *Saccharomyces cerevisiae* species. Top fermentation tends to be quite vigorous, generating considerable heat; a week or so is enough for most British brews.

Top Hat Burtonwood's bottled and keg strong ale (1046) from Cheshire. A man in a top hat used to be the brewery symbol.

Top Island Randalls Vautier keg best bitter (1042) from the largest of the Channel Islands, Jersey.

Top Pressure The use of carbon dioxide under pressure to force beer up from the cellar to the counter fitting. Spoils the beer flavour by allowing too much gas to dissolve.

Topsy Turvy Berrow Brewery strong ale (1055) from Somerset.

Top-up A request to a barman to fill the glass to the correct level so as to receive a full measure. In British law it is necessary to ask for a top-up and be refused, before proceeding with a complaint of short measure.

Tower Bass cask bitter (1036) in the north, from Tadcaster. Formerly known as Brew Ten.

Tower Brewery The classical 19th-century style of brewery, built as a narrow tall building. Arranged internally so that after the malt and water are raised to the topmost floors, materials then flow downwards from process to process by gravity. Many such buildings are still readily identifiable although their original use has long since changed.

Traditional As applied to beer, 'traditional' has no definable meaning (as opposed to 'real ale' and 'cask conditioned'). If it is accepted that a practice continued for a generation (30 years) constitutes a tradition, then the brewing of lager in Wrexham and Alloa since the 1880s is 'traditional'. As applied to British breweries, 'traditional' implies that the processes of ale brewing are followed: eg use of the infusion mash tun rather than lauter tun or decoction systems, use of open fermenters, and no final processing (filtration, pasteurisation, recarbonation).

Trappist Strong top-fermenting, bottle-conditioned ales produced by the five Trappist abbeys of Chimay, Orval, Rochefort, St Sixtus, and Westmalle in Belgium and Schaapskooi in the Netherlands.

Traquair House Unique brewery set in Scotland's oldest continually inhabited house in Peeblesshire, where the Laird of Traquair recommenced brewing a rich dark ale in 1965 in 200-year-old vessels. Has since added a weaker draught beer.
Cask: Bear Ale (1050). *Bottled*: Traquair House Ale (1075) – occasionally found on draught.

Treble Gold Friary Meux's bottled strong ale (1052) brewed by Ind Coope at Burton.

Treble Seven Gales keg dark mild (1034) from Hampshire.

Trent Allied's bottled take-home bitter (1032) and mild (1033), named after their Burton-upon-Trent brewery.

Tripel A very distinctive golden Trappist ale (8 per cent alcohol) produced by the Abbaye of Westmalle.

The style has been copied by commercial Belgian brewers using the Tripel name.

Triple Crown Usher's light keg bitter (1033), also sold as a Mann's brand.

Triple X Hermitage premium bitter (1044) from West Sussex. See also *XXX*.

Trophy Whitbread's national keg bitter (1035), which has now largely been replaced in the south by Best Bitter. Brewed by Fremlins, Samlesbury, Salford, and Sheffield. A lower-gravity version (1033) is brewed at Cheltenham, and a stronger Special (1040) at Castle Eden. Cask Trophy (1037) is also now being tried in the north.

Trough Bradford brewery set up in 1981, now brewing its value-for-money beers for five tied houses. *Cask beers*: Bitter (1035.9), Wild Boar (1039).

TROUGH

Trub Solid malt protein formed during boiling of the wort, which is removed prior to fermentation.

Truman Reputably Britain's oldest brewery, dating back to 1666. Watney's London partner in Brick Lane still runs its own 900 pubs in the southeast with their own range of beers. *Cask*: Bitter (1036), Best Bitter (1045), Sampson (1055). *Keg*: Prize Brew (1032), Special Mild (1032), Special Bitter (1035), Bitter (1036), Ben Truman (1038). *Bottled*: Light Ale (1032), Brown Ale (1032), Ben Truman (1045), Brewers Gold (1078), Barley Wine (1086).

TSB Tooley Street Bitter (1040) from London – not to be confused with the Trustee Savings Bank!

Tube Australian term for a can of beer.

Tuborg The internationally-known Danish brewery which with Carlsberg makes up United Breweries of Copenhagen. In Britain, Tuborg Pilsner (1030) and Gold (1045) are brewed at Carlsberg's Northampton brewery and sold under franchise by a number of regional breweries including Vaux, Burtonwood, and Everards. Vaux also brew Tuborg.

Tudor Ale Liddington's premium cask bitter (1044)

from Rugby. Also Gale's bottled beer (1051).

Tulip Lees light bottled lager (1034) from Manchester, one of the first British-brewed 'lagers' with the then popular Dutch image.

Tun Originally a very large cask of several hundred gallons but now only used as a name for various brewery vessels, eg Mash Tun.

Tun Bitter Creedy Valley cask ale (1041) from Crediton, Devon.

Tut See *Shive*.

Twelve Horse A strongish American ale (5 per cent alcohol) produced by Genesee of Rochester, New York.

250 Tolly Cobbold's strong bottled pale ale (1073), first brewed in 1973 to celebrate 250 years of brewing in East Anglia.

Two-rowed Barley Barleycorns that grow in two-rowed ears, the most common variety found in the UK. Compare *Six-rowed Barley*.

Twyford Amber Bottled ale brewed by Guinness at Park Royal, London, for export only.

Tyke West Riding's award-winning best bitter (1041) from Huddersfield.

[U]

U Fleku Famous Prague home-brew pub producing its own Czechoslovak dark lager (5.4 per cent alcohol).

Ullage Waste beer, such as beer drawn off from pumps before serving, beer left in the cask, spillage, etc. Most brewers give publicans an 'ullage allowance'. However, some unscrupulous landlords filter ullage beer back into good casks.

Umbrella A structure within the copper that looks like a large mushroom. It operates rather like a coffee percolator: boiling wort rises up the central column and cascades out over the domed top, thus ensuring very vigorous mixing of the copper's contents.

Under-age drinking Illegal consumption of liquor by those under the legal minimum age, which is 18 in the UK. It is also an offence for adults to supply under-18s with liquor.

Underback When the mash is complete the wort, containing the dissolved malt sugars, is run off into the copper. This run-off is via the underback, a vessel that does some filtering and is also often used to dissolve any brewers' sugar that is to be added to the brew.

Unicorn The sign of Robinson's ales from Stockport.

Union See *Burton Union*.

United Breweries The giant company of Denmark which includes Carlsberg and Tuborg, and is linked with the Rupert Group of South Africa.

Ur *or* **Urtyp** German word meaning 'original', faithfully adopted only by breweries which created a beer style (eg Spaten Ur-Marzen or Pilsner Urquell). A pity that British breweries are not so precise.

Usher Watney's West Country brewery, with 680 pubs, at Trowbridge, Wiltshire. *Cask beers*: PA (1031), Best Bitter (1038), Founder's Ale (1045). *Keg*: Triple Crown (1033), Country Bitter (1036). *Bottled*: Brown Ale (1032), Light Ale (1034), Winter Ale (1060). *Can only*: Ploughman's Bitter (1032).

[V]

Varsity Morrell's premium cask and keg bitter (1041) from Oxford.

Vat A large vessel in a brewery, more usually an open one such as a fermenting vessel.

Vault North of England alternative to the Public Bar; originally the room where the casks were stored.

Vaux Britain's second largest regional brewing group, based in the northeast, with a total of 730 pubs and breweries in Scotland (Lorimer), South Yorkshire (Darley and Ward), and even Belgium (Liefmans), besides Sunderland. *Cask beers*: Sunderland Draught

(1040), Samson (1042). *Keg*: Mild (1033), Original Pale (1033), Sunderland (1040), Samson (1042), Tuborg (1030), Frisk (1033). *Bottle*: Coopers Bitter (1032), Original Pale (1033), Double Maxim (1044), Norseman (1032). See also *Lorimer*, *Darley*, *Ward*, and *Liefmans*.

VB Vauxlaurens Brewery. See *Randall*.

Velvet Courage and Webster's bottled stout (1042).

Vent Release of the excess carbon dioxide built up in a cask owing to the secondary fermentation. The gas is released slowly via a soft spile. See *Spile*.

Verticillium Wilt See *Wilt*.

Victoriana A style of decor much loved by modern interior designers, intended to recall the days of the Gin Palace, characterised by dark timber, mirrors, and pseudo-gas lamps. Sometimes achieved at great expense in pubs whose original Victorian features were ripped out a decade previously.

Victory Ale Paradise Brewery's strong rich ale (1070) from Cornwall.

Victualler Traditionally a purveyor of food. Hence, licensed victualler should refer to a purveyor of food and alcoholic beverages.

Vienna A stronger copper-coloured lager style created in Austria's capital, but popularised over the border in Germany where it is known as Marzen.

Viking Morland's bottled pale ale (1042) from Abingdon. Also once the name of Devenish's lager.

Village Light cask bitter (1035) from Archers of Swindon.

Vintage beers Not only wine improves with age; so do a few beers, notably strong Belgian bottle-conditioned ales. Blue-capped Chimay is best after two years but can be kept for five. Liefmans Provisie also reaches a peak after two years but matures for another 25. In Britain, Courage year-dates its Imperial Russian Stout and Eldridge Pope recommend their Thomas Hardy Ale be kept for five years.

VPA Burt's Ventnor Pale Ale or Best Bitter (1040) from the Isle of Wight, one of the best-value cask beers in Britain at its price and gravity.

[W]

Wadworth Classic country family brewery in Wiltshire whose Northgate Brewery and mighty dray horses have dominated the market town of Devizes since 1885. Real ales of character, still from wooden casks, in almost all 142 pubs, but best known for their famous 6X in the free trade. *Cask beers*: Devizes Bitter (1030), IPA (1034), 6X (1040), Farmers Glory (1046), Old Timer (1055). *Keg*: Northgate Bitter (1036), Raker Bitter (1030). *Bottled*: Brown Ale (1030), Light Ale (1030), Extralite (1030), Green Label (1040), Old Timer (1052). Also canned Best Bitter (1040) and Bitter Ale (1030).

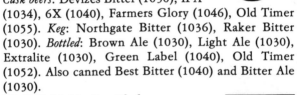

Wakefield Ale See *Clark*.

Walker Peter Walker subsidiary of Tetley Walker, formed in 1981 to run 76 highly traditional pubs, mainly on Merseyside. All serve real ales specially brewed by Tetley Walker at the Warrington brewery founded by Peter Walker in 1824. *Cask beers*: Walker Mild (1032), Bitter (1033), Best Bitter (1035.5). *Keg*: Bergman's Lager (1033). *Bottled*: Brown Peter (1034).

Wallop Bourne Valley's special winter brew (1056) from Hampshire, named after a London slang word for beer.

Wanderhausen From the German 'Wandering House'; a modern malting system employing huge moving trays, an adaptation of the Saladin Box system.

Wangford Arms Suffolk's first home-brew pub, set up in Wangford in 1985. *Cask beer*: Wangle (1040).

Wards Sheffield brewery with 100 pubs, part of the Vaux Group since 1972, as are fellow South Yorkshire brewers, Darley of Thorne. *Cask beers*: Mild (1033),

Sheffield Best Bitter (1038). *Keg*: As cask.

Warrington Brown See *Old Chester*.

Warrior Home-brew pub in Brixton, London. *Cask beers*: Brixton Bitter (1036), Best (1040), Warrior (1050).

Wassail Ballard's strong brew (1060) from Sussex, named after the old English name for a festive drinking session.

Water See *Liquor*.

Water Engine A machine mounted on pub cellar walls that converts ordinary mains water pressure into compressed air for use in air-pressure beer dispense, using a series of slide valves. Only a few engines remain in active use, in Scotland.

Watney Combe Reid London-based company running 1,500 pubs in the southeast and the Stag Brewery at Mortlake. *Cask beers*: Antler (1035), Combes Bitter (1041), Stag (1044). *Keg*: Special Mild (1032), Starlight (1033), Light Mild (1034), Antler (1035), Special Bitter (1037), Carlsberg (1030), Foster's (1035), Holsten Export (1045). *Bottled*: Brown Ale (1032), Pale Ale (1033), Cream Label Stout (1038), Strong Export (1048), Export Gold (1070), Stingo (1076).

Watney Mann Truman Brewing division of hotel and leisure giant, Grand Metropolitan, formed after Britain's biggest takeover battle in 1972 when Grand Met. seized Watneys for £413m. Operates six breweries in London (2), Wiltshire, Yorkshire, Manchester, and Scotland, having closed its Norwich brewery in 1985. Runs 5,000 pubs through nine regional companies: Drybrough of Edinburgh, Manns of Northampton, Norwich of East Anglia, Phoenix of Brighton, Truman and Watney of London, Ushers of Trowbridge, Websters of Halifax, and Wilsons of Manchester. The last two merged in 1985. 1,800 managed houses are run by the associated Host Group and Berni and Clifton Inns. Grand Met. also owns two breweries abroad: Maes of Belgium and Stern of West Germany.

WB Cask bitter (1037) from Cotleigh Brewery, Somerset, chiefly brewed for the New Inn, Waterley Bottom, Glos.

Weavers Cask bitter (1037) from Bourne Valley Brewery, Hampshire.

Webster Watney's brewery in Halifax with 280 pubs, whose Yorkshire Bitter has become almost a national beer. Also has a major lager brewing plant for Carlsberg, Fosters, Budweiser, etc. *Cask beers*: Dark Mild (1032), Light (1034), Yorkshire Bitter (1037.5). *Keg*: Dark Mild (1032), Green Label Best (1034), Pennine Bitter (1037), Yorkshire Bitter (1037.5). *Bottled*: Sam Brown (1034), Yorkshire Bitter (1037), Green Label (1038), Velvet Stout (1042).

Wee Heavy Scottish term for a nip-sized bottle of strong ale. Name first used for Fowler's Wee Heavy, the famous 1110 OG brew of John Fowler of Prestonpans, East Lothian.

Wee Willie Younger's bottled brown and pale ales (1032). Name chiefly used in Northern Ireland.

Weihenstephan This Bavarian brewery at Freising is reputedly the oldest in the world, dating back to 1040. Now linked with the State-owned Hofbrauhaus, it co-operates with Bavaria's institute of brewing, notably to produce Weizen (wheat) beers.

Weisse Means white beer, and usually refers to the top-fermented pale brews of Berlin (see *Berliner Weisse*.) Similar beers are produced elsewhere in Germany, and also to the east of Brussels in the village of Hoegaarden.

Weizen Means wheat beer originating from South Germany, using much more wheat in the mash than the Weisse (white) beers of Berlin. They are also stronger and come in a variety of styles from Hefeweizen (with sediment) and filtered Hefefrei (yeast-free) to strong Weizenbocks, some bottom-fermented, others top. Notable Weizen brewers are Hofbrauhaus, Sanwald, and Weihenstephan.

Wells Bedford family brewery, best known as Charles Wells, which completely rebuilt its brewery on a fresh site in the mid-1970s. Has 275 pubs, including a growing number in London. *Cask beers*: Eagle Bitter (1035), Bombardier (1042). *Keg*: Mild (1030), Silver Special (1030), Gold Eagle (1034), Noggin (1039), Kellerbrau (1034), Red Stripe (1044). *Bottled*: Light (1030), Bowman Brown (1030), Bitter (1034), Double Star (1040), Fargo (1046), Old Bedford (1078), Kellerbrau (1034), Red Stripe (1044). Also for export: Bowman Strong (1054), Angler's Lager (1054).

Welsh Bitter Whitbread's weak keg bitter (1032) for Wales. Brewed at Magor.

Welsh Brewers Bass's Welsh company with 500 pubs and a brewery in Cardiff. Sometimes still trading under the old Hancock name. *Cask beers*: Worthington Pale (1033), Hancock's PA (1033), Worthington M (1033), Worthington Dark (1034), Hancock's HB (1037), Worthington BB (1037), Fussell's Best (1038). *Keg*: Allbright (1033).

Wem Largely untouched Shropshire subsidiary of regional giant Greenall Whitley, producing a fine range of real ales at the brewery near Shrewsbury for all their 200 houses. *Cask beers*: Pale Ale (1033), Mild (1035), Best Bitter (1038), Special (1042). See also *Greenall Whitley*.

Wembley Wilson's bottled pale ale (1036) – from Manchester.

Wessex Devenish cask best bitter (1042) from Weymouth, Dorset. Bottled as Wessex Pale Ale.

West Country Whitbread's low-gravity cask pale ale (1030), brewed at Cheltenham.

Westmalle The most unusual Belgian Trappist beer, Tripel, is brewed at this Abbaye on the Dutch border. There is also a darker 'double'.

West Riding Award-winning small brewery set up in Huddersfield in 1980 and now, after a fire, brewing at Meltham. One pub. *Cask beers*: Best Mild (1033), Dark Mild (1033), Bitter (1037), Tyke (1041), Special (1050).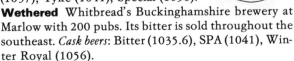

Wethered Whitbread's Buckinghamshire brewery at Marlow with 200 pubs. Its bitter is sold throughout the southeast. *Cask beers*: Bitter (1035.6), SPA (1041), Winter Royal (1056).

Wet Rent The traditional method of renting a pub to a tenant: the building was rented for a very low, almost nominal, sum and then most of the brewery's income was by way of a surcharge on the wholesale price of the drink – the wet rent. This has now largely given way to very much higher rents on the property.

Wharfdale Special cask ale (1045) from Goose Eye, Yorkshire.

Wherry Woodforde's best bitter (1039) from Norfolk, named after the flat-bottomed boats of the Broads.

Whirlpool See *Centrifuge*.

Whitbread National brewer with 6,800 pubs, which has heavily rationalised its breweries during the early 1980s. In 1981 it ran 16; three years later that number was halved, with plants closing in Hampshire (2), Kent, Devon, Cardiff, Liverpool, Leeds, and Luton. This was largely due to the opening of two huge megakeggeries at Magor, South Wales, and Samlesbury, Lancs. Whitbread now has only six remaining traditional breweries: Castle Eden, County Durham; Chesters, Salford; Flowers, Cheltenham; Fremlins, Kent; Wethereds, Bucks; and Sheffield. National brands – *Keg*: Best Mild (1032), Trophy (1035), Tankard (1037), Best Bitter (1038), Heineken (1033), Stella Artois (1047). *Bottled*: Light Ale (1032), Forest Brown (1032), Pale Ale (1034), English Ale (1042), Brewmaster (1042), Mackeson (1042), Gold Label (1098).

Whitbread Investments Whitbread, whose other interests include Stowells Wines, Threshers off-licences, and Long John whisky, also controls a sister investment company which has major stakes in many 'independent' British breweries. The main holdings are: Morland (40%), Marston (35%), Brakspear (27%), Devenish (26%), Boddington (22%), Buckley (18%), Border (17%). The holdings in Border and Marston assisted the takeover of the Welsh company in 1984 by Marston. Investments has also acted to prevent take-overs, notably helping Davenports ward off Banks's in 1983.

White Beer See *Weisse*.

White Shield Worthington's famous bottle-conditioned beer (1051) from Bass, which requires a whole art to itself to pour if you want to avoid the sediment.

Wild Beer See *Lambic*.

Wild Boar Trough's best bitter (1039) from Bradford.

William Younger Scottish & Newcastle's southern England and South Wales marketing company.

Wilmot's Hop Cone Godson's cask bitter (1042), named after an early partner in the East London brewery.

Wilson Watney's Manchester brewery with 720 pubs, the vast majority serving real ale. *Cask beers*: Original Mild (1031.5), Original Bitter (1036.5). *Keg*: Mild (1031), Special Mild (1031), Newton Bitter (1032), Pale (1033.5), Bitter (1036), Great Northern (1036). *Bottled*: Brown Ale (1031), Pale Ale (1032), Wembley (1036), Winter Warmer (1055), Top Brass lager (1033). In 1985 merged with neighbouring Watney subsidiary, Webster.

Wilt A disease (full name Verticillium Wilt) affecting hops which has led to the development of new wilt-resistant varieties like Target.

Wiltshire Gibbs Mew's cask and keg special bitter (1036) from Salisbury.

Wine Bar Licensed premises where wine is the staple drink, of historic origin (eg El Vino's, the Fleet Street haunt of journalists); now widely used to describe trendy food-and-drink bars.

Winkles Small North Derbyshire brewery set up in a former bomb factory in Buxton in 1979, now concentrating on its family chain of tied houses. *Cask beers*: Saxon Cross Mild (1037), Bitter (1037), BVA (1037).

Wino Slang term for an alcoholic.

Winston This very English-sounding beer (7.5 per cent alcohol) is produced in Belgium, where strong 'English' ales are a speciality. Odder still, the ones that are imported, like Martin's Pale Ale from Courage, are often unheard of in Britain.

Winston's Stout Patriotically-named strong stout (1053), especially brewed by Belhaven of Scotland for export to Italy. Despite the title, the bottle label features Mary, Queen of Scots!

Winter Ale See *Old Ale*.

Winter Reserve Hilden's stronger winter ale (1044)

from Northern Ireland.

Winter Royal Fine, warming winter draught (1056) from Wethereds, Marlow, Bucks.

Winter Warmer Young's draught brew (1055) to help London drinkers through the chillier months.

Witney Cask bitter (1037) from Glenny's brewery, Witney, Oxon.

Woodforde Norfolk brewery begun in 1981 in Norwich before moving to the Spread Eagle, Erpingham, in 1983. *Cask beers*: Norfolk Pride (1036), Wherry (1039), Norfolk Porter (1041), Old Norfolk (1043), Phoenix XXX (1047).

Woodham Cask bitter (1035.5) from Crouch Vale, Essex.

Woods Small brewery begun in 1980 behind the Plough Inn, Wistanstow, Shropshire, but now supplying over 50 free trade outlets. *Cask beers*: Parish (1040), Special (1043), Christmas Cracker (1060).

Woodsman Keg dark mild (1034) from New Forest brewery, Hants.

Wort The liquid, containing all the extracts from the malted grain, that will subsequently be fermented into beer. The extract run off from the mash tun is the *sweet wort*; after boiling with the hops it is the *hopped wort*.

Worthington Famous Burton brewer who merged with Bass in 1927. The brewery has since been demolished but the name survives on various beers, notably Worthington White Shield, the naturally-conditioned bottled beer (1051), and a variety of cask beers in South Wales (see *Welsh Brewers*). Also keg Bitter (1036), 'E' (1041); bottled Light (1032), Export (1041).

Wowser Australian term for a non-drinker or killjoy.

Wrexham The oldest lager brewery in Britain, founded in 1882 and taken over by Ind Coope in 1949. Still brews Wrexham Lager for North Wales, although now specialises in brewing foreign lagers under licence for Allied. *Keg*: Long Life (1040), Wrexham Lager (1033), Oranjeboom (1033), Bergman's (1033), Castlemaine XXXX (1035), Skol (1037), Lowenbrau (1041), Skol Special (1046). *Bottled*: Wrexham Export (1046). *Canned only*: Long Life (1040), Long life Export (1046).

Wychwood Premium cask bitter (1044) from Glenny of Oxfordshire.

[X]

X 17th-century excisemen used a cross to denote the single- (X) or double-strength (XX) wort (see *Strong Ale*). The practice spread; its original purpose was lost, and it became a (dubious) claim of strength and quality, with brewers marking their casks XXX, XXXX, or even XXXXXX. The number of Xs today does not indicate any regular measure of strength.

XB Four outstanding real ales from four northern breweries – Bateman's bitter (1036), Hartley's best bitter (1040), Theakston's premium ale (1045), and, from Scotland, Devanha's heavy (1036).

XS Clark's strong winter ale (1052) from Wakefield. Not to be drunk to 'XS'!

XX Greene King's cask dark mild (1031) from East Anglia. A similar brew under the same name is produced by Harveys of Sussex (1030). Also Shepherd Neame keg light mild (1033).

XXX Common name for a wide variety of beers. Cask milds from Donnington (1034), Brakspear (1030), and Ridley (1034). Cask bitters from Paines (1036) and the Three Tuns home-brew pub (1042). Unusual dark, malty brew (1042) from Devanha. See also *Triple X*.

XXXB Bateman's powerful, malty cask bitter (1048) from Wainfleet, near Skegness, introduced in 1977 chiefly for the free trade outside Lincolnshire. Now bottled as Ploughman's Ale.

XXXD Gales cask dark mild (1032) from Horndean, Hampshire.

XXXL Gales sister beer to XXXD, a cask light mild (1030).

XXXX Milds from Bass (1031), Sam Smith (1033), and St Austell (1034), besides draught old ales from Brakspear (1043), Harveys (1043), and King & Barnes

(1046). See also *4X*.

XXXXX Gales dark winter brew (1044) from Horndean, Hampshire. See also *Five X*.

XXXXXX See *6X* and *Sixex*.

[Y]

Yard of Ale A long glass vessel (holding between 2¼ and 4½ pints), used for drinking contests, with a surprise for the unwary in its bulbous end. If it is tilted too sharply, beer will flood over the drinker's face.

Yeast A microscopic single-celled plant able to metabolise carbohydrate. The waste products excreted by the plant include alcohol and carbon dioxide together with many more complex organic chemicals. Yeasts come in many strains and, while all produce alcohol, the mix of the other chemicals varies so that different yeasts produce different flavours. In the past, brewers just kept yeast from one brew to start the next, and so on indefinitely; as most of the yeasts are mixtures of different strains, and the mixtures can change with time, this can give rise to changes in the resulting beer. It is now common practice to propagate single strains from one selected cell. These yeasts may be used for a number of brews and then a new batch will be propagated to keep the strain pure. In addition to the beneficial yeasts, there are multitudes of wild yeasts whose spores exist everywhere. These yeasts will generally spoil any beer they infect, although in Belgium these are used to brew a unique beer called Lambic. See also *Saccharomyces*.

Yeoman Greene King's paler keg bitter (1038) from East Anglia, named after a hop variety.

Yorkshire Name given to keg and cask bitters from the county when sold in the south, notably John Smith's (1036) and Webster's (1037.5).

Yorkshire Grey Clifton Inns home-brew pub, Holborn, London. *Cask beers*: Headline Bitter (1037), Holborn Best (1047).

Yorkshire Square See *Square*.

Young London's famous independent family brewers who stood alone against the keg tide in the Capital in the early 1970s. Real ale in all 144 pubs, some delivered by horse-drawn drays around the Wandsworth brewery. *Cask beers*: Bitter (1036), Special (1046), Winter Warmer (1055). *Keg*: Bitter (1036), London Lager (1037), Premium (1047). *Bottled*: Pale Ale (1030), Brown Ale (1030), Ram Rod (1046), Export (1062), Old Nick (1084), London Lager (1037).

Younger The old 'Father William' half of Scottish Brewers. See *Scottish & Newcastle*.

Yuengling The oldest brewery in the United States, in Pottsville, Pennsylvania, dating back to 1829, and known for its 'celebrated' Pottsville Porter.

[Z]

Zum Uerige Famous old home-brew house at 1 Bergerstrasse, Düsseldorf, West Germany, producing the unique German dark ale, Alt.

Zymamonas See *Rope*.

Zymurgy The art and science of brewing. Also the name of the American home-brewers' magazine.